Simple Crocheting

A Complete How-to-Crochet Workshop with 20 Projects

Erika Knight

St. Martin's Griffin
New York

Editorial director Jane O'Shea
Creative director Helen Lewis
Project editor Lisa Pendreigh
Pattern checker Sally Harding
Designer Claire Peters
Design assistant Nicola Davidson
Photographer Yuki Sugiura
Stylist Charis White
Models Chinh Hoang, Kim Lightbody,
and Panda
Illustrators Joy Fitzsimmons
and Paul Griffin
Production director Vincent Smith
Production controller Aysun Hughes

For information, address St. Martin's
Press, 175 Fifth Avenue, New York,
N.Y. 10010.

www.stmartins.com

Printed in China.

Library of Congress Cataloging-in-
Publication Data Available Upon Request

ISBN 978-1-250-01621-8

First U.S. Edition: November 2012

10 9 8 7 6 5 4 3 2 1

It is the simplicity of crochet that inspires me. With just a few basic stitches worked either in lines or round and round, using only a hook and some yarn you can create seemingly endless textures. With only one stitch ever in work on the hook, it is a deceptively simple craft that anyone can master, as well as being conveniently portable.

I love the craft of crochet for its diversity; from the fabulously fine filet and imitating intricate lace of traditional crochet to the extremely oversized contemporary motifs made from the fattest yarns. Over the years, I have collected it all: old-fashioned afghans, vintage edgings, kitsch kitchen accessories, and now the rejuvenated crochet motifs that are currently enjoying a fashion moment on the catwalks, fueling the revival of this fabulous craft.

The projects in this book, *Simple Crocheting*, are very much my take on crochet. This book is not intended as an exhaustive "wikipedia" on the minutiae of crochet. Instead it is a simple introduction to the craft, to set you on your way to mastering basic techniques, selecting yarns, and considering color palettes. I have pared down the craft to the essentials as I see them with the aim of providing the means to get you crocheting. I believe in conquering just the few working methods that are easy, effective, and give the right look I require for a specific design. *Simple Crocheting* is crochet my style.

For me, crochet is about the process as well as the project. In the Materials and Techniques section at the start of this book, I have set out the technical how-to information for the basic crochet methods and stitches, but knowing how to work a particular technique is no use in isolation and really only makes sense once it is put into practice. This is where the Project Workshops come in. In fact, providing you can master the simple techniques of making a foundation chain, working the basic stitches, and grasping the concept of turning chains, then you can easily make the first few items in the Project Workshops section of this book. There are twenty projects in all, including essential accessories and timeless homewares—from the basic starter project of a thrifty dishcloth suitable for the beginner crocheter to the more challenging laceweight scarf and colorful patchwork-inspired motif throw.

Each project provides the chance to practice and perfect a specific technique or two courtesy of a masterclass. It's your choice whether you work your way through the projects sequentially, refining your skills with each masterclass, or dip in and out of the projects at will—either way you will soon become adept at working the basic stitches, shaping with simple increases and decreases, creating enhanced textures with puff stitches, bobble stitches, and popcorn stitches, and joining in different colors.

Throughout *Simple Crocheting*, all of the projects reflect my personal preference for an unfussy style; simple shapes generally with no extraneous embellishment in which the texture and shade of each yarn—natural fibers and muted color tones—are integral to my designs. I am, however, exacting about how I make up the final piece: it is essential to take the time to finish a project. But again this doesn't have to be difficult. I have given instructions for the three best methods of seaming together pieces of crochet.

As well as honing the skills given in the Materials and Techniques section and practiced in the Project Workshops, I hope that you will enjoy the variety of textures and patterns that can be created with crochet. In the Stitch Library I have included sixteen of my very favorite stitches and motifs. Again, I hope you will be inspired to experiment with different stitch textures and experiment with colors in order to create your own style.

I love the entire process of creating and constructing a crocheted fabric. This book, *Simple Crocheting*, is my interpretation of the craft. I hope that you will share my love for the pastime and, within these pages, find the inspiration to pick up that hook and simply crochet.

Skill levels

In reality, all the projects in this book are unashamedly simple—that's my style. However, each project has been attributed with a skill level in accordance with the Craft Yarn Council of America's rating system in order to let you know what techniques you are mastering as you learn to crochet.

BEGINNER

1 Beginner Projects For first-time crocheters using basic stitches. Minimal shaping.

EASY

2 Easy Projects Using basic stitches, repetitive stitch patterns, simple color changes, and simple shaping and finishing.

INTERMEDIATE

3 Intermediate Projects Using a variety of techniques, such as basic lace patterns or color patterns, and mid-level shaping and finishing.

EXPERIENCED

4 Experienced Projects With intricate stitch patterns, techniques, and dimension, such as non-repeating patterns, multicolor techniques, fine threads, small hooks, detailed shaping, and refined finishing.

materials and techniques

Choosing yarns and colors

Yarn has always been an integral part of my work, whether as a consultant to the fashion industry or working within the craft worlds of hand knitting and crochet. When devising a project, the sourcing of materials is always my starting point where the yarn—or, indeed, the fiber—sets the course the project is to take.

With yarns that range from the whisper-fine to the phenomenally fat, I love the extremes that the craft of crochet allows. Whatever yarn I select, a yarn must be "fit for purpose" or "right for the job" as it determines the color, stitch pattern, and texture of the final fabric and therefore informs the entire character of the project. In an exhaustive and exacting process, I swatch up each yarn to accurately analyze how it performs and looks. This is not only one of the most crucial parts of designing but, for me, it is also one of the most pleasurable. It is often a protracted task as I can spend hours playing with texture through fibers, trying to capture the essence of yarns in a design sketch on paper with my HB pencil.

The time invested in this early design stage is, I believe, always repaid as the quality of yarn is inherent in everything I do. This is particularly paramount when creating very simple pieces: how the yarn handles on the crochet hook, the fluidity or firmness of the resulting fabric, how the fabric will hang or drape, all of this must work together for a project to be truly successful. For many makers, the choice of yarn is either an overlooked part of the process as they speed to the prize of the finished project or is entrusted wholly to the prescriptive pattern instructions.

From string to cashmere, I love the performance of natural fibers. I tend to use natural yarns because of their inherent characteristics—they keep the wearer warm in winter yet cool in summer, wicking moisture away from the skin. Moreover natural fibers are soft, comfortable to wear, and not without the hint of luxury that comes only from wearing nature's finest.

For the projects in this book, I have chosen a variety of yarns for their unique textures. Primarily, I have selected animal fibers, including the softest baby alpaca, robust extra-fine merino wool, pure British wool as well as voluminous light-weight wools. Alongside these luxurious animal fibers, sit a small selection of the best natural plant fibers: the versatile staple, mercerized cotton, and the most ancient of the plant fibers, the exquisite linen.

As with selecting fibers, when choosing colors my natural inclination is to steer toward natural shades. The soft tones characteristic of natural yarns enhance the understated simplicity of what I aim to achieve in my designs and provide a solid base to any palette. That said, perversely, I also love to play with "pops" of stronger color that add energy to an overall color scheme. I find this approach works particularly well when designing for the home. In fact, putting together a color story now feels like second nature to me. The Stripe Pillows on pages 64–67, for example, incorporate "pops" of teal, fuchsia, and chartreuse to enliven on otherwise neutral background of brown, ecru, and taupe.

Likewise, throws provide a great opportunity to work with random and eclectic colors to create an individual statement piece. Alternatively, for an elegant timeless heirloom that would suit most sensibilities, throws can be worked in several toning shades or, for the more color-confident, a striking, dynamic two-color palette never fails, black and ecru being my favorite. But let's not forget the naturally exquisite single color, which can instantly become a classic piece. Color dilemmas we all identify with, no doubt.

Not only am I passionate about designing with yarns, I also believe in promoting the natural, sustainable origins of wool. In creating my Erika Knight Yarn Collection, I am supporting both the British hill farmers and the British textile industry while at the same time creating the ultimate hand-knitting yarns in British wool.

09 brooches

Yarns: fine

The cyclical nature of fashion has seen lace return to the fore. Laceweight and other fine yarns are becoming increasingly popular as gossamer-spun silks and mohairs create contemporary yet classic shawls, scarves, and throws. Crochet originally emulated intricate medieval lacework, exquisite textiles in fine cotton and linen threads. Edgings, accessories, and homewares were especially popular; one can only covet these pieces, which now mainly reside in textile galleries.

Right Fine and classic crochet linen; its inherent characteristic is its ancient, natural beauty. Linen yarn is an absolute favorite of mine. (Anchor Artiste Linen); **Below** A crochet classic, mercerized cotton, its subtle sheen and compact surface creates firm, precise stitches (Yeoman Yarns Cotton Cannele 4-Ply); **Opposite (from top to bottom)** An alpaca–merino blend yarn (Rowan Fine Lace), delicate and ethereal, tones with two shades of mercerized cotton (Yeoman Yarns Cotton Cannele 4-Ply).

 Yarn weight: lace
lace, fingering, and 10-count crochet thread
Average crochet gauge: 32–42 double crochet stitches to 4 inches
Recommended hook sizes: 6 steel to B-1 (1.5–2.25mm)

 Yarn weight: super fine
sock, fingering, and baby
Average crochet gauge: 21–32 single crochet stitches to 4 inches
Recommended hook sizes: B-1 to E-4 (2.25–3.5mm)

 Yarn weight: fine
sport and baby
Average crochet gauge: 16–20 single crochet stitches to 4 inches
Recommended hook sizes: E-4 to 7 (3.5–4.5mm)

(These are the most commonly used gauges and hook sizes for these yarn categories.)

Yarns: medium

Probably the most popular of all yarn weights, medium yarns are easy to work with and readily available. This range consists of double knitting, light worsted, aran, worsted, and afghan weight yarns. Over the years, medium yarns have been the entry route to crochet for many crafters. Medium-weight yarns are generally smooth to work with and give good stitch clarity, yet often they can create a less fluid fabric. With crochet especially, it is great to experiment with different weights of yarn using the same stitches to achieve just the right fabric.

 Yarn weight: light
double knitting and light worsted
Average crochet gauge: 12–17 single crochet stitches to 4 inches
Recommended hook sizes: 7 to I-9 (4.5–5.5mm)

 Yarn weight: medium
aran, worsted, and afghan
Average crochet gauge: 11–14 single crochet stitches to 4 inches
Recommended hook sizes: I–9 to K-10½ (5.5–6.5mm)

(These are the most commonly used gauges and hook sizes for these yarn categories.)

Above (from left to right) My very own worsted spun aran-weight wool in hanks (Erika Knight Vintage Wool); **Opposite (clockwise from top left)** A glorious jumble of medium-weight yarns, including a pure baby-alpaca yarn (Rowan Baby Alpaca DK), a cotton-and-silk-blend yarn (Rowan Savannah), and a chain yarn consisting of a blend of merino, baby alpaca, and nylon (Rowan Lima).

Yarns: fat

I have always created my own yarns by cutting lengths of woven material and plying together several ends of different textures, twisting them to give a more inspiring thread. This is a great way to recycle surplus natural fabrics or use up stash yarns in an eclectic fashion. Ingrid Wagner has pursued this further and re-energizes waste products of the textile industry by using the selvage edges of looms to great and dramatic effect with huge crochet hooks. The working of crochet on such a large scale creates a whole new vibrancy and way of seeing when working with familiar stitches and fabrics. I have used Ingrid's gorgeous big yarn, worked on a size U (25mm) hook, to create a simple and homely round rug (see pages 100–3). Similarly, working traditional crochet motifs in my own voluminous Maxi Wool, the simple kimono-shape jacket has taken on the appearance of extreme lace (see pages 136–41).

Opposite Finer yarns (**top**) can be plyed together to create a fat "supa" yarn by simply working with two or three strands together; make a continuous yarn (**bottom right**) by cutting fabric into strips (see masterclass, page 102), this is made easier if the fabric is washed beforehand to remove any stiff dressing applied in the manufacturing process; a chunky weight pure wool yarn (**left**) from my own collection (Erika Knight Maxi Wool); **Above** A unique blend of 100% totally British wool, which has been steam finished to enhance its volume, softness, and handle (Erika Knight Maxi Wool).

 5 Yarn weight: bulky
chunky, craft, and rug
Average crochet gauge: 8–11 single crochet stitches to 4 inches
Recommended hook sizes: K–10½ to M–13 (6.5–9mm)

6 Yarn weight: super bulky
super chunky, bulky, and roving
Average crochet gauge: 5–9 single crochet stitches to 4 inches
Recommended hook sizes: M-13 (9mm) and larger

(These are the most commonly used gauges and hook sizes for these yarn categories.)

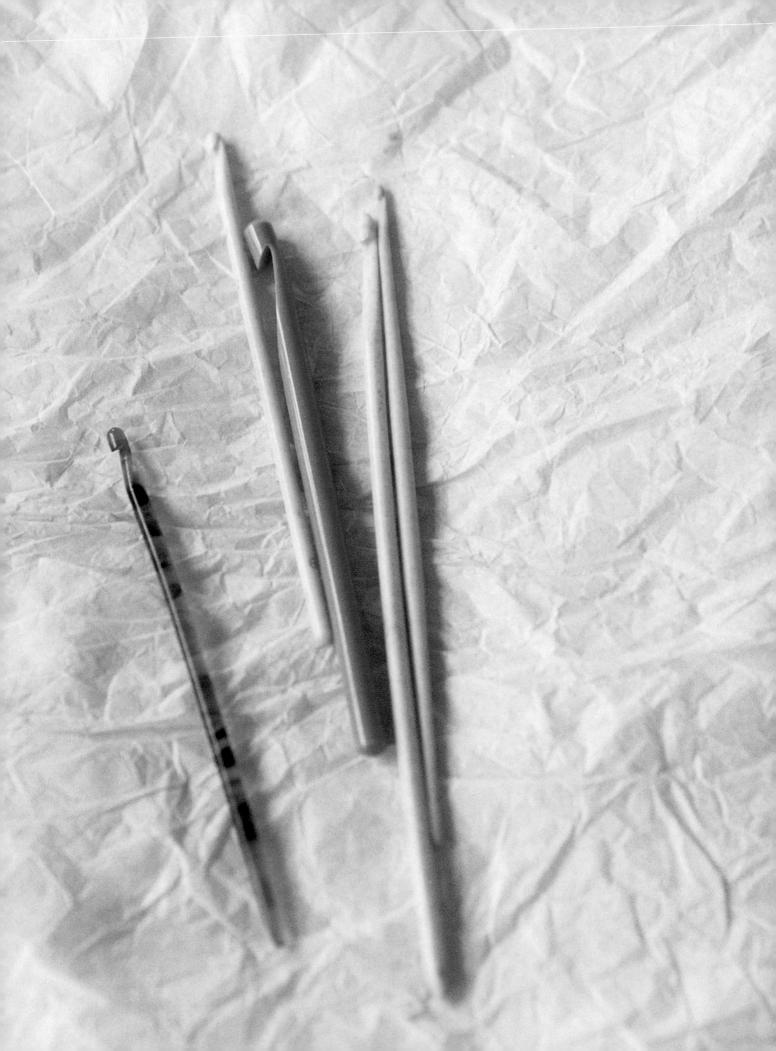

Equipment

You require only the minimum amount of equipment fo crochet, but one of the most important tools is your crochet hook. Hooks come in a variety of materials and you should choose the kind that feels comfortable and works well with your chosen yarn.

Hooks A crochet hook is a deceptively simple, yet perfectly designed, piece of equipment. The handle is long enough to extend comfortably across your fingers when the hook is held in the right position and balances the whole hook. The grip is the flattened area that you hold between your thumb and index finger. The size of the hook is printed on the grip. The shank is the part between the grip and the hook and its diameter determines the size of the hook. The throat is the bend under the tip that catches the yarn. The tip is smooth and rounded and enables you to slip the hook into the stitch smoothly. Basic hooks come in a variety of sizes from a size 4 steel to an N/P-15. Smaller steel hooks for lace work start as small as a 14 steel (.60mm) and go up to a size 00 (2.7mm).

Aluminum and plastic Hooks are most commonly made from aluminium and in the basic shape described above. You will find a good range

of sizes in aluminum but the larger sizes are often made in plastic as they would be too heavy if made in aluminium. Gray opaque plastic is the most common material although you can find hooks in brightly colored plastic, which are either translucent or opaque. Plastic feels warmer to the touch and is slightly flexible.

Steel Small size hooks are often made in steel as this material gives a finer finish and greater strength. These are the type of hook you should choose if you are working with fine cotton.

Wood and bamboo Wooden hooks are made from hardwood and sometimes have decorated handles. They are heavier than fine-grained bamboo. Both these finishes are less common than aluminum, plastic, and steel and can be less smooth.

Sizing Hooks are measured in millimeters and this measurement is taken around the shank of the hook. To measure a hook for yourself, slip the shank into the holes of a size gauge until you get a snug fit. Measurements can vary slightly depending on the manufacturer, which is another reason why you should always crochet a gauge square before you begin a piece of crochet and check that you are using the correct size.

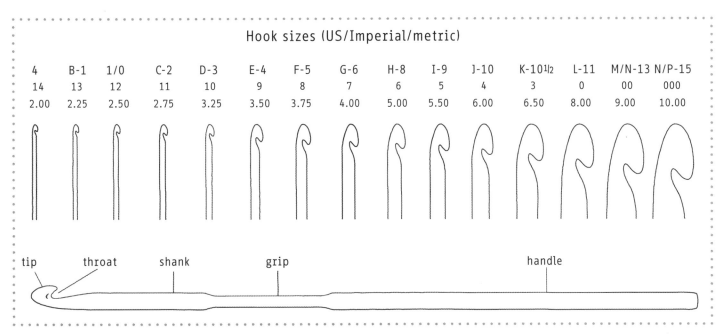

Hook sizes (US/Imperial/metric)

4	B-1	1/0	C-2	D-3	E-4	F-5	G-6	H-8	I-9	J-10	K-10½	L-11	M/N-13	N/P-15
14	13	12	11	10	9	8	7	6	5	4	3	0	00	000
2.00	2.25	2.50	2.75	3.25	3.50	3.75	4.00	5.00	5.50	6.00	6.50	8.00	9.00	10.00

tip   throat   shank   grip   handle

Making a slip knot

To begin to crochet, you need to make a slip knot on the hook. Unlike knitting, there is only ever one stitch on the hook at any one time and the slip knot is the starting point for all stitches that go to make up the finished work.

1 About 6 inches from the end of the yarn make a loop by taking the short end over the yarn and then letting the end hang down behind the loop formed.

2 Insert the hook from right to left under the yarn and draw it through the loop, as shown.

3 Pull down on both ends of the yarn. The knot will slide up and tighten around the hook.

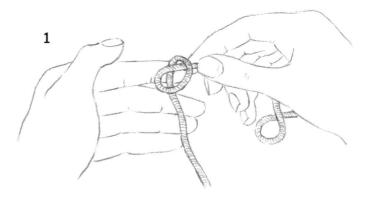

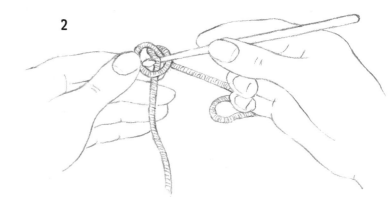

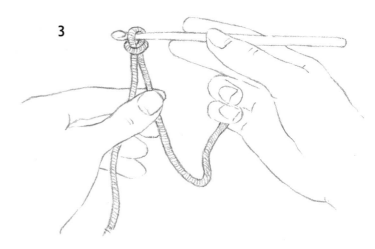

Holding the hook

Crochet is so simple because all you need to do is hold one hook and work one stitch at a time. There are two ways to hold the hook, so try out both of them and see which you find more comfortable.

Pencil grip
Hold the hook as if it were a pencil. Grasp the flat part of the hook between your thumb and index finger and have the stem resting across the curve between your thumb and index finger.

Knife grip
Hold the hook as if you were using a knife. Grasp the flat part of the hook between your thumb and index finger but have the back of your hand on top of the hook with the stem under your palm.

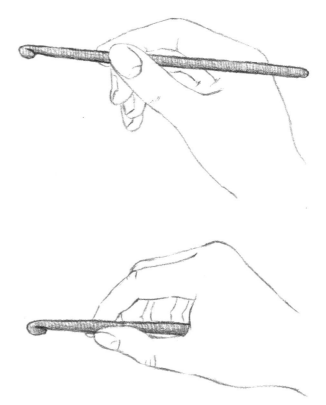

Left-hand method

Crocheting with the left hand is exactly the same as with the right hand but with the hook and yarn position reversed; hook in the left hand, yarn wrapped around the right hand.

Controlling the yarn

The way you hold the yarn allows it to flow from the ball with the right amount of tension. There are two methods to try: the index finger method and the middle finger method. Again, try both of them and see which you find most comfortable.

Index Finger Method

1 Hold the hook with the slip knot in your right hand. Take the working yarn (the end attached to the ball) between the little finger and the next finger and wrap it clockwise around your little finger.

2 Take the yarn under the next two fingers and over and around the index finger.

3 Hold the yarn, beneath the slip knot, between the thumb and middle finger of your left hand. Now raise your index finger. You are now ready to crochet, working with the yarn between the hook and your index finger.

1

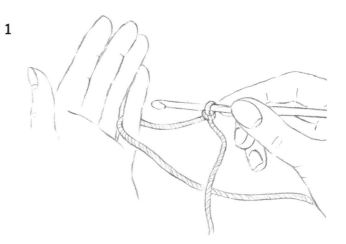

2

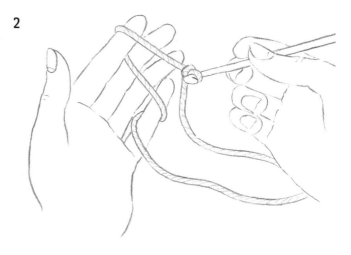

3

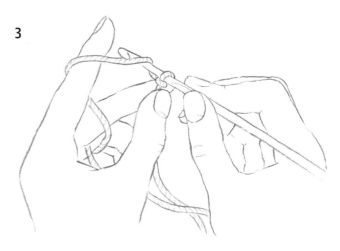

Middle Finger Method

1 Hold the hook with the slip knot in your right hand. Take the working yarn (the end attached to the ball) between the little finger and the next finger and wrap it clockwise around your little finger.

2 Take the yarn across your other fingers and over the top of your index finger.

3 Hold the yarn, just below the slip knot, between the thumb and index finger of your left hand. Now raise your middle finger to control the yarn and pull it through your fingers. You will be working with the yarn between the hook and your middle finger.

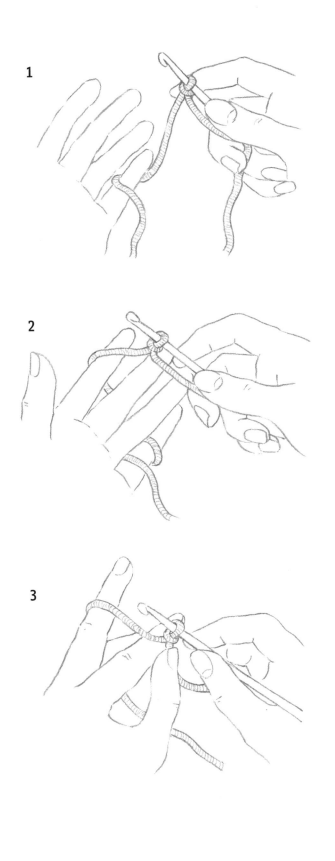

1

2

3

Tensioning the tail

It is necessary to apply some tension to the tail end of the yarn, otherwise you'll find yourself attempting to crochet in mid air. Use either the second or the third finger and thumb of your left hand to pull gently on the tail end of the yarn by pinching it just below the hook.

Making a foundation chain

Crochet most often starts with a series of chain stitches, which are used to make the first row: this is called the foundation chain. It needs to be worked loosely and evenly to ensure that the hook can enter each loop on the first row. You may find it tricky to keep an even yarn tension at first but, again, you may need to practice this several times.

1 Holding the slip knot with the left hand and keeping the yarn taut between the hook and your raised finger, push the hook forward and twist it toward you as you take it under, behind, and then over the yarn so that the yarn wraps around the hook and is caught in the slot. This is called yarn over hook (abbreviated yo).

2 Draw the yarn through the loop on the hook, keeping the yarn under an even tension. This forms a new loop on the hook and makes one chain stitch. The new loop should be loose enough to allow the next chain to be drawn through easily.

3 Holding the chain nearest the hook with the thumb and middle finger, repeat steps 1 and 2 until you have the required number of chains. Do not count the loop on the hook. All the chain stitches should be the same size.

1

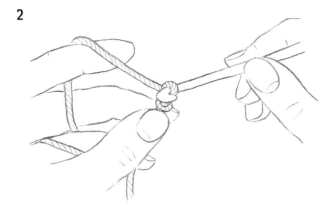

2

3

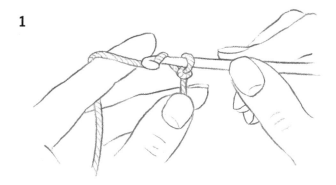

Counting chains

When working from a pattern you will need to work a given number of chains to create the foundation row. It is therefore important that you can recognize the formation of each chain and thus count correctly.

The front of a chain
This front of the chain looks like a series of V shapes made by the yarn. Each V is a chain loop sitting between a chain loop above and a chain loop below. The first chain at the beginning will have the slip knot sitting directly underneath it. The surface of the chain is smooth on this side. Stitches should be counted from this side of the chain where possible.

The reverse of a chain
The reverse of the chains has a row of bumps that have been created by the yarn. These bumps sit behind the V and run in a vertical direction from the beginning of the chain up to the hook. The surface of the reverse of the chain is more textural than the front side.

Counting chains
When counting the chains you do not count the stitch that sits on the hook. This is because a loop will remain on the hook up until the moment you fasten off. To making counting easier when creating a large number of chains it may be a good idea to use stitch markers at a predetermined interval, say after every 10 or 20 stitches.

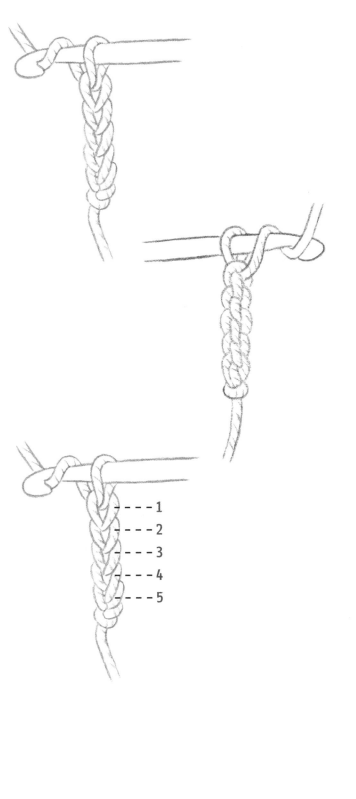

1
2
3
4
5

:Working loose stitches

When making chain (or subsequent) stitches you must make sure that each stitch is taken up onto the thicker part of the hook (the shank) before starting the next one. If you work your stitches on the thinner part of the hook (the throat) they will become tight, and you will struggle to place your hook into them on subsequent rows.

Working slip stitch

There are five basic stitches used within crochet. Slip stitch is the most basic of all those five. It is used mostly for joining rows when you are working in the round and for decreasing. However, it is an excellent stitch to start with and for you to practice the skills of holding the hook and the yarn.

1 Make a foundation chain of evenly worked chain stitches. Identify the second chain from the hook.

2 Insert the hook from front to back under the top loop of the second chain.

1

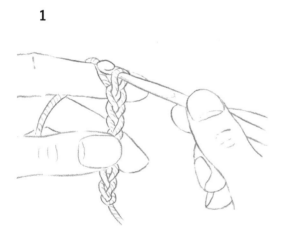

2

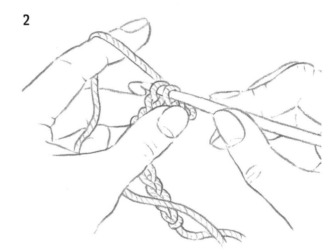

3 Take the hook under, behind, and then over the yarn (yarn over hook—yo) so the yarn is caught by the hook.

4 Draw the yarn back through the two loops now on the hook. You will now have one loop on the hook and this completes the slip stitch.

5 To continue working slip stitch, insert the hook into the next chain and repeat steps 3 and 4.

3

4

5

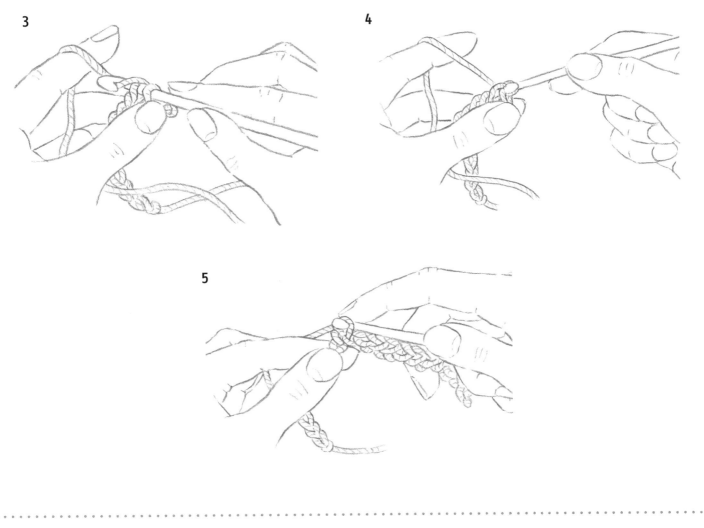

Working single crochet

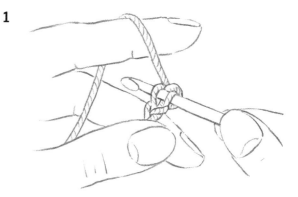

Single crochet is a core stitch to learn. Once mastered, single crochet and the other basic stitches can be used in combination to make a variety of decorative stitches. Single crochet is one of the easiest basic stitches.

1 Once you have worked the foundation chain, identify the second chain from the hook. Insert the hook from front to back under the top loop of the second chain.

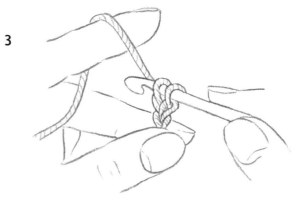

2 Take the yarn over the hook.

3 Draw the yarn back through the first loop on the hook. You will now have two loops on the hook.

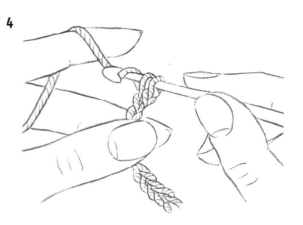

4 Take the yarn over the hook.

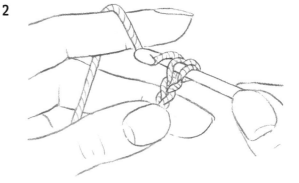

5 Draw the yarn through both loops on the hook. You now have one loop on the hook and this completes the stitch.

6 Work one single crochet into each chain of the foundation chain. At the end of the row, turn the work so the yarn is behind the hook. Work one chain stitch. This is called the turning chain and does not count as a stitch (see page 36).

7 Insert the hook from front to back under both top loops of the first single crochet at the beginning of the row.

8 Work a single crochet into each stitch of the previous row. Make sure you work into the last single crochet stitch of the row below but not the turning chain.

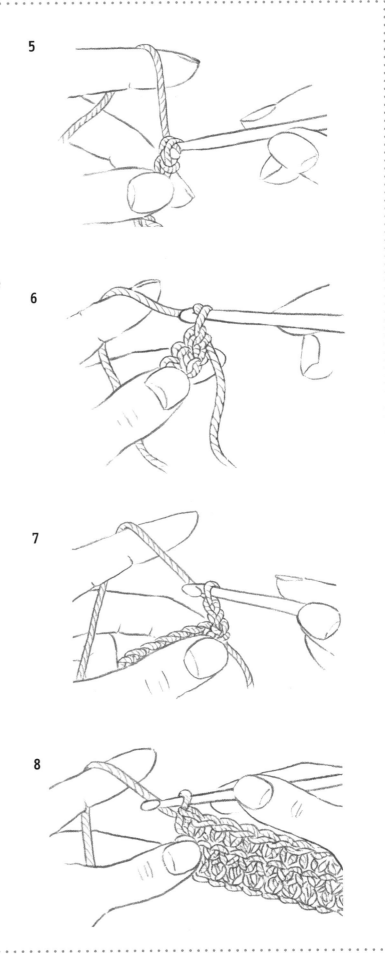

5

6

7

8

Turning chain
For single crochet
All rows—one chain to turn and then insert hook into first stitch.

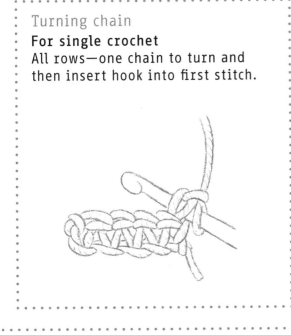

Working half double crochet

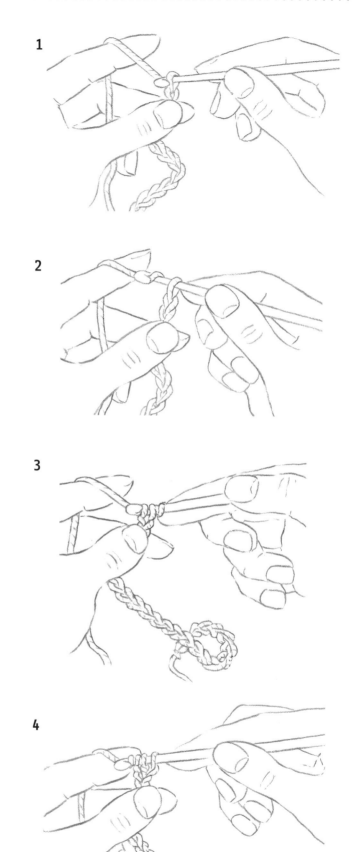

1

2

3

4

A half double crochet is between a single and a double crochet in height. The stitch produces a fabric that is less firm than single crochet, but not as open as double crochet, with an attractive ridge across the fabric. The abbreviation for half double crochet is hdc.

1 Make a slip knot about 6 inches from the end of the yarn and insert the hook from right to left. Make a foundation chain.

2 Once you have worked the foundation chain, take the yarn over the hook. Identify the third chain from the hook.

3 Insert the hook from front to back under the top loop of the third chain.

4 Take the yarn over the hook and draw it back through the chain loop. You will now have three loops on the hook. Take the yarn over the hook and draw it through the three loops. This completes the first half double crochet.

5 Continue in this way, working a half double into each chain to the end of the row.

6 Turn the work and make a turning chain of two chains. This counts as the first half double of the next row.

7 Skip the first stitch at the base of the turning chain and work a half double under both loops of the second stitch in the previous row.

8 Continue in this way, making a half double into each stitch of the previous row including the top of the turning chain from the previous row.

5

6

7

8

Turning chain
For half double crochet
Foundation row—miss two chains at beginning of foundation row. Subsequent rows—two chains to turn and then insert hook into second stitch.

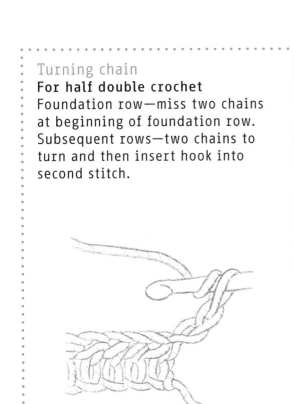

Working double crochet

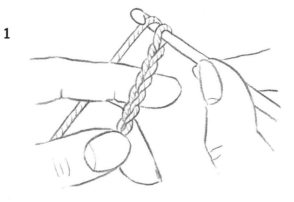

The third of the five basic stitches is double crochet. Double crochet stitches are twice as tall as single crochet stitches and work up quickly to form a more open fabric. Double crochet is the basis of many patterned stitches. The abbreviation for double crochet is dc.

1 Make a slip knot about 6 inches from the end of the yarn and insert the hook from right to left. Make a foundation chain. Once you have worked the foundation chain, take the yarn over the hook. Identify the fourth chain from the hook.

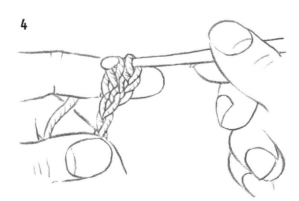

2 Insert the hook from front to back under the top loop of the fourth chain.

3 Take the yarn over the hook and draw it back through the chain loop. You will now have three loops on the hook.

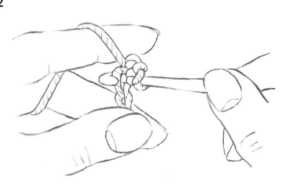

4 Take the yarn over the hook and draw it through the first two loops on the hook. You will now have two loops on the hook.

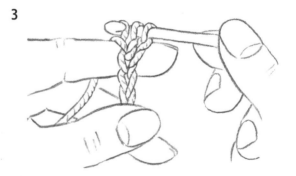

5 Take the yarn over the hook again. Draw the yarn through the remaining two loops on the hook. You will now have one loop on the hook and the stitch is complete.

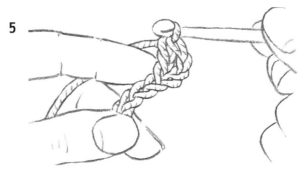

6 Continue along the foundation chain, working a double crochet in each chain. This completes one row of double crochet.

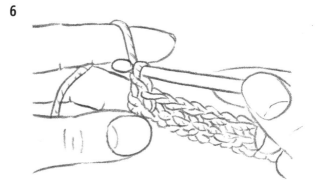

7 To begin the next row, turn the work and make a turning chain of three chain stitches. This turning chain counts as the first stitch of the row. Now locate the second double crochet stitch in the previous row.

8 Take the yarn over the hook and insert the hook from front to back under BOTH loops of this second stitch. Repeat steps 3–5. Continue along the row, working a double crochet under both loops of each double crochet in the row below. When you reach the end of the row, work the last stitch into the top chain of the turning chain on the previous row.

Turning chain
For double crochet
Foundation row—miss three chains at beginning of foundation row. Subsequent rows—three chains to turn and then insert hook into second stitch.

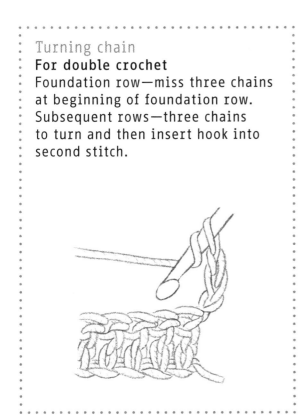

Working treble crochet

This crochet stitch is three times as tall as a single crochet and forms an open fabric with a looser texture. The abbreviation for treble crochet is tr.

1 Make a slip knot about 6 inches from the end of the yarn and make a foundation chain. Once you have worked the foundation chain, take the yarn over the hook twice. Identify the fifth chain from the hook. Insert the hook from front to back under the top loop of the fifth chain. Take the yarn over the hook.

2 Draw the yarn back through the chain loop on the hook. You will now have four loops on the hook.

3 Take the yarn over the hook. Draw it through two loops only. There are now three loops on the hook.

4 Take the yarn over the hook. Draw it through two loops only. There are now two loops on the hook.

1
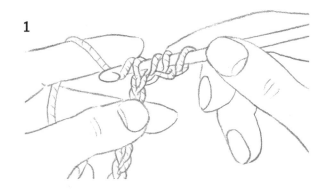

2
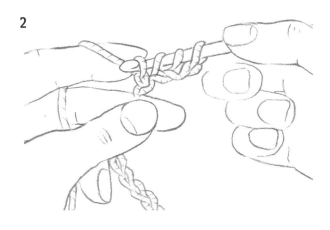

3
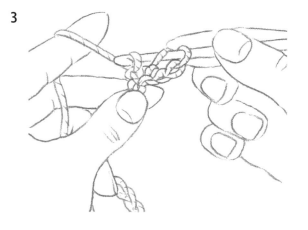

4
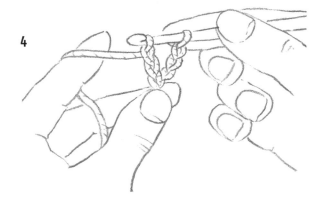

5 Take the yarn over the hook. Draw it through the remaining two loops. You now have one loop on the hook and this completes the stitch.

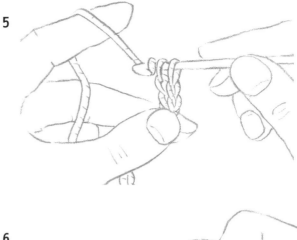

6 Work one treble crochet into each chain of the foundation chain.

7 When you reach the end of the row, turn the work so that the yarn is behind the hook. Work four chain stitches. This turning chain counts as the first treble of the new row. You are now ready to work back in the other direction.

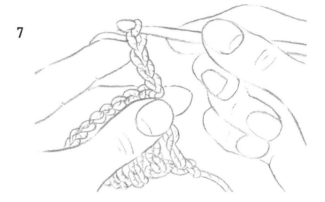

8 Skip the first stitch at the base of the turning chain. Work a treble into the second stitch inserting the hook under both the top loops of the stitch in the previous row. Continue in this way, working a treble crochet into each stitch to the end, including the top chain of the turning chain.

Turning chain
For treble crochet
Foundation row—miss four chains at beginning of foundation row. Subsequent rows—four chains to turn and then insert hook into second stitch.

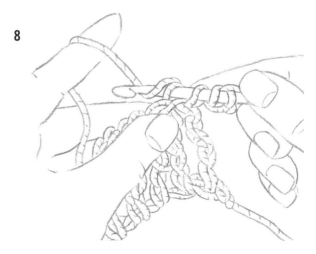

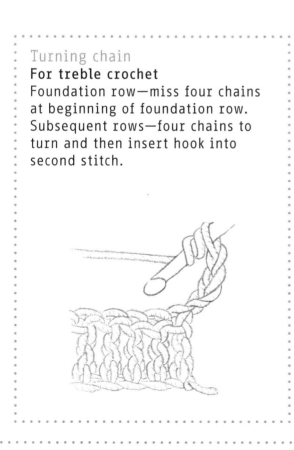

Working turning chains

When crochet is worked in rows and the work is turned between each row you must add turning chains to bring the hook up to the height of the new row of stitches. Each crochet stitch uses a specified number of chains because the stitches vary in height. You can make a turning chain in two ways and both are explained here.

Turning chain counts as first stitch
1 This is the most common way of making a turning chain. Work to the end of the first row and turn the work. Make the number of chains as instructed in the pattern. Identify the second stitch of the row below, as you are going to work into this, skipping the first stitch.

2 Insert the hook from front to back under the top two loops of the second stitch in the row below. By skipping the first stitch you have made the turning chain the first stitch of this new row.

3 Work to the end of the row, making a stitch into the top of every stitch on the row below. When you reach the end, make the last stitch into the top of the turning chain from the row below. Working in this way keeps the number of stitches constant and the edges of the work straight.

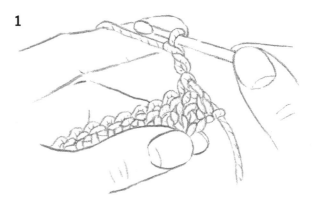

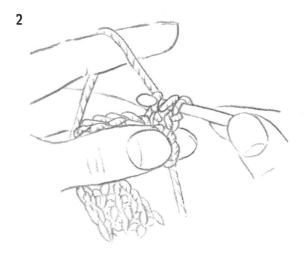

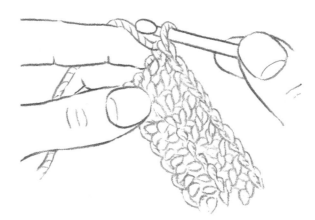

Turning chain does not count as a stitch

1 This method is used for short stitches, such as single crochet. Work to the end of the row and turn the work. Make the number of chains as instructed and identify the first stitch at the beginning of the row.

2 Work the first stitch into the first stitch at the base of the turning chain. Continue to the end of the row and work the last stitch into the last single crochet of the row below, not the turning chain.

1

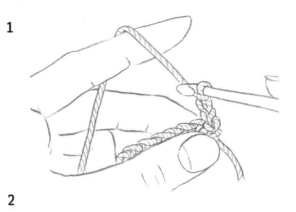

2

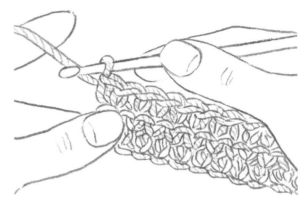

When to turn

You can add the turning chains at the end of the row, before you turn the work, or after you have turned the work and before you begin the new row. Adding at the end makes it easier to count the chains if you need to double check, while many patterns will instruct you to add at the beginning—the choice is yours.

Adding at the end

1 When you reach the end of the row, work the number of chains required and then turn the work. You must turn it from right to left so the yarn is behind the hook in this way you do not twist the chain.

Adding at the beginning

1 When you reach the end of the row, turn the work so the yarn is behind the hook and then add the required number of chains.

1

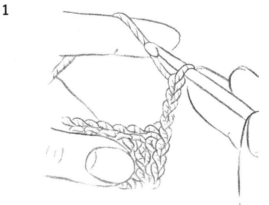

2

Working in the round

Instead of working backward and forward
in horizontal rows, you can work crochet by
starting with a central ring and continuing
outward in rounds. When working in rounds,
the right side of the work is facing you at all
times. The shape of the round is dictated by the
decreases and increases that are made as you
work the round.

1 Make a short foundation chain of six chains
or as instructed in the pattern. Join the chains
into a ring by working a slip stitch into the first
chain of the foundation chain.

2 Work a starting chain for the first round. The
number of chains worked depends on the stitch
being used. For double crochet, for example, you
will need to work three chains and this counts
as the first double.

3 Now work the first round of the pattern.
Work the stitches into the center of the ring by
inserting the hook into the space in the center
of the ring each time and not into the loops on
the foundation chain.

1

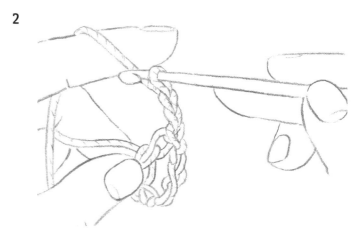

2

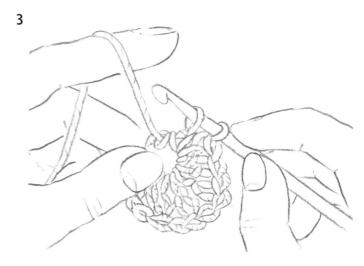

3

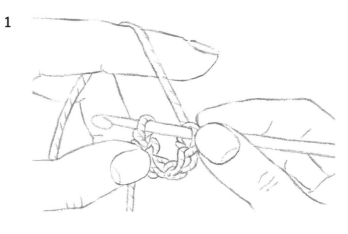

4 To complete the round, you need to join the first and last stitches of the round together. To do this for a round of double crochet, for example, work a slip stitch into the third chain of the starting chain as shown.

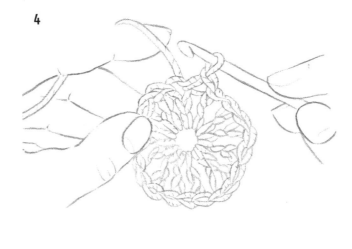

5 Make the starting chain for the next round. For double crochet, work three chains, which again counts as one double. To continue, work one double into the same place. Now work two doubles into each stitch of the previous round. Increasing in this way makes a circular shape. Complete the round by working a slip stitch into the third chain of the starting chain to join the first and last stitches. Working each round as instructed, the number of stitches in each round is increased so that the circle of stitches grows in size.

Working into spaces

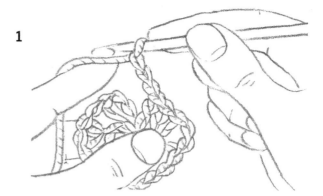

The effects of many crochet designs are formed not just by the stitches but also by where they are placed and the spaces around them. When following a pattern it is often necessary to work into a space made in the previous row or round, rather than working into or around the stitch. Similarly, skipping a stitch or two is often integral to a design, particularly if you are working a lacy crochet fabric.

When creating a textured effect by varying the placement of the stitches, the actual stitch being worked is made in exactly the same way as normal—it is only the point where the hook is inserted through the previous rows or rounds that varies. The pattern will state how to place the stitches. Working into the top of a stitch is most common, but working between stitches into the space between them is often called for.

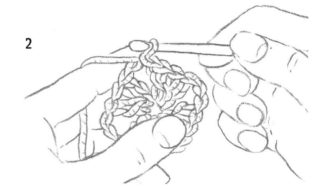

Working into spaces on a square motif

1 Make a foundation chain and slip stitch into the first chain to form a ring. Make 5 chains (this counts as 1 double and 2 chains). *Work 3 doubles into the ring and then make 2 chains.*

2 Repeat from * to * twice more then work 2 doubles into the ring. Join with a slip stitch to the third of the 5 chains made at the beginning.

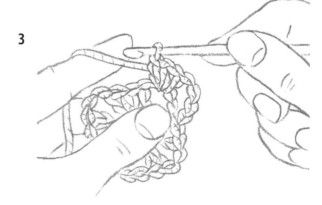

3 Slip stitch into the next 2-chain space, make 4 chains, then work 3 half doubles into the same 2-chain space.

4 **Make 1 chain, skip 3 doubles and then work 3 half doubles, 2 chains, and 3 half doubles into the next 2-chain space.** Repeat from ** to ** twice more. Make 1 chain, skip 3 doubles and work 2 half doubles into the same space as the four chains at the beginning of the round. Join with a slip stitch to the second chain of the four chains. Continue working rounds in this way following your instructions.

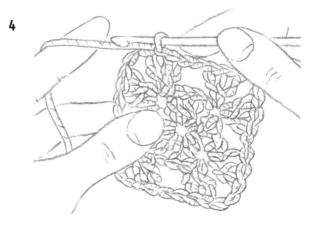

Checking your gauge

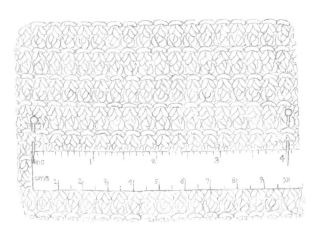

It is important to check your gauge before you embark on any project. Gauge is the number of stitches and rows across a particular measurement. The gauge determines the measurements of a project, so it is important that you obtain the same number of rows and stitches as the pattern states.

If your gauge differs from that stated in the pattern, your finished piece may be a different size or a distorted shape. A small difference over 4 inches can add up to a considerable amount over the complete width of the crocheted item. If your gauge is looser or tighter than the one stated in the pattern, a garment will be larger or smaller than the specified size. So taking time out for 15 minutes to work a gauge square before you start can save a lot of heartache later on.

The size of the stitch depends on the type and weight of the yarn, the size of the hook, the stitch being worked, and your control of the yarn. It can also depend on mood—many crocheters will have experienced a tighter gauge when stress levels are high!

Making a gauge swatch
Using the same yarn and hook and stitch that the gauge has been measured over in the pattern, crochet a sample at least 5 inches square.

Measuring a gauge swatch
Smooth out the square on a flat surface. To check stitch gauge, place a ruler (a cloth tape measure can be less accurate) horizontally on the fabric and mark 4 inches with pins. Count the number of stitches between the pins. To check row gauge, place a ruler vertically, mark 4 inches with pins and count the number of rows.

Correcting your gauge
If the number of stitches and rows is greater than it says in the pattern, your gauge is tighter. This can usually be regulated by using a larger hook. If the number of stitches is fewer than the specified number, your gauge is looser and you should change to a smaller hook.

A word of caution: your gauge may change from that of your sample when crocheting the actual garment, as your crochet gauge can alter when working across more stitches. If you are finding it impossible to match the gauge stated in the pattern, it is more important to match the stitch gauge than the row gauge. You can always compensate for the row gauge by working more or fewer rows as necessary.

Finishing and seaming

Always take time to finish off your crochet carefully. Here are explanations for what your instrucions mean by "fastening off" and "darning in ends," plus a few seaming techniques. There are several ways to join pieces of crochet together, either with a sewing needle or a crochet hook and three of the most popular are given here. For seaming, use the same yarn or a finer yarn matching the project color.

Fastening off

Once you have finished crocheting any piece, you need to fasten off your work securely.

1 When you have finished the final row or round you will be left with one loop on the hook. Cut the yarn approximately 12 inches from the hook. Wrap the cut yarn around the hook and draw it through the loop on the hook.

2 Remove the hook and pass the yarn end through the loop. Pull on the end of the yarn to tighten the knot.

Darning in ends

To get rid of any ends that have not been "enclosed" by working over them, darn the working end of the yarn neatly into the back of the work as shown. Then clip off the yarn end close to the crochet fabric.

1

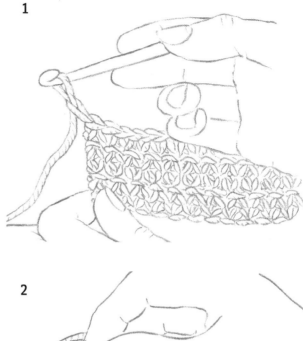

2

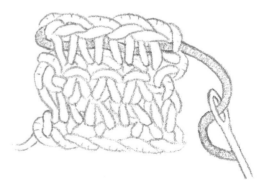

Slip stitch seam

Worked with a hook, the slip stitch seam is a popular method of joining pieces. Place the two pieces to be joined together with the right sides facing. Insert the hook through both pieces at the beginning of the seam, yarn over hook and draw through both pieces and the loop on the hook. Working through both layers slip stitch across the rest of the seam. Take care not to work too tightly as although it is strong and secure, it can be quite rigid and create a slightly bulky seam.

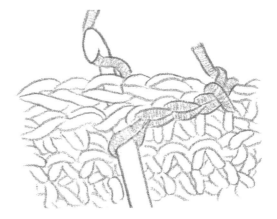

Single crochet seam

A single crochet seam is good for joining straight edges as it makes a less bulky seam. It can also be worked on the right side of the fabric and so can be used to make a feature. It also has the advantage of being slightly stretchy. Place the pieces to be joined together with either right or wrong sides together, as preferred. Insert the hook from front to back through the edges of both pieces, yarn over hook and draw through, complete one single crochet in the usual way and then insert the hook into the next stitch ready to make the next single crochet. Continue in this way to the end of the seam and then fasten off.

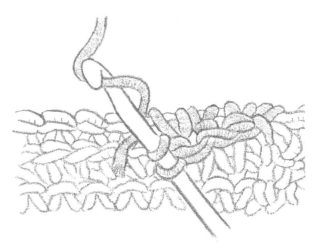

Woven seam

Worked with a blunt-ended needle, I prefer to use a woven seam mostly to give a flatter finish as the straight sides are joined edge to edge. With the right sides of both pieces facing up and the edges to be seamed lined up row to row or stitch to stitch, insert the needle up through the right side of the stitch at the beginning of the seam on piece one. Next insert the needle from the bottom of the stitch to the top of the first stitch at the beginning of the seam of piece two. Then insert the needle up through the next stitch of piece one and then through the second stitch of piece two. Repeat this "zigzag" process until the seam is completed. Carefully tighten the tension of the stitches as you work so the edges slowly pull together.

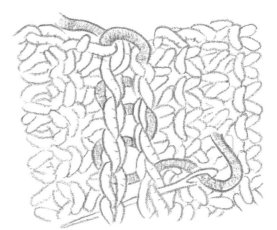

Understanding patterns

When it comes to understanding crochet patterns, there are many shared conventions and terminology. Though designers may use slight variations in style, the same information is always given. Before purchasing yarn for any project, read through the pattern to ensure you understand exactly what is needed.

Size

For homewares and accessories, patterns usually come in a single size. For garment designs, often a choice of sizes ranging from extra small to extra large are given. Sometimes sizes are given as "to fit"—the recommended chest or bust measurement for each size—and sometimes they are given as "actual"—the measurements of the finished crocheted piece. Depending on the intended fit of a garment, whether it is loose or tight fitting, these two measurements vary by a certain number of inches.

Materials

The pattern specifies what type of yarn is needed for the project, along with the total number of balls. The Asymmetric Cardigan on pages 132–137 is a one-size garment designed to be loose fitting, but when other patterns are for garments that come in different sizes, the number of balls needed for each size will be stated. Also given in the materials list will be the size of crochet hook or hooks required, which could be one or more, as well as any closures, such as buttons and zippers, or trims.

Gauge

The gauge indicates how many stitches and rows you must have to a certain measurement, usually 4 inches square. Your gauge needs to be correct to achieve the exact dimensions given in a pattern (see page 41 for more on this). Achieving an exact gauge is less important for a throw or a pillow than for a garment, when a different gauge will not only affect the finished dimensions but will alter the amount of yarn needed to complete the project.

Pattern instructions

Crochet patterns can be either written or given in a symbol diagram. Sometimes the diagram replaces the written words completely or it is given as well as the line-by-line instructions. The pattern works through the individual elements of the project, giving all the necessary instructions for each part. Every pattern begins with the hook size, shade (or shades) of yarn used, and the number of chains worked for the foundation row or ring. The pattern continues to outline, row-by-row or round-by-round, the stitch pattern to follow and indicates when any shaping or other details, such as buttonholes, should be worked. Follow the instructions for each row or round carefully, paying particular attention to the turning chains.

Abbreviations

The names for stitches and instructions are abbreviated otherwise the patterns would be too long and too difficult to follow. The list of abbreviations is given at the beginning of the pattern and you should check these to make sure you understand each one. It can take a while to become familiar with the language of crochet patterns, so I have listed opposite the most commonly used abbreviations and symbols.

Brackets and parentheses

When following a pattern, you need to be aware of the different usage of parentheses ( ) and brackets [ ]. Parentheses are used to contain additional instruction or clarification, such as, ch 3 (counts as first dc). Brackets are used when a direction has to be repeated a certain number of times; for example, [1 dc in each of next 2 sts, ch 4] 3 times.

Asterisks

These are used to make patterns shorter and are placed at the beginning of a set of instructions to be repeated. A single asterisk marks the beginning of a pattern repeat sequence. For example, *ch 2, skip 2 ch, 1 dc in next ch; rep from * to end. A double asterisk often indicates a repeat within a series of instructions.

Abbreviations

Following is a list of the most commonly used abbreviations within crochet patterns. In addition, special abbreviations may also be included at the start of a pattern, such as the directions for a specific stitch, which are not necessarily on this list.

alt	alternate
approx	approximately
beg	begin/beginning
CC	contrasting color
ch	chain(s)
cl	cluster(s)
cm	centimeter(s)
cont	continue/continuing
dc	double crochet(s)
dec	decrease(s)/decreasing
dtr	double treble(s)
foll	follow(s)/following
g	gram(s)
hdc	half double crochet
inc	increase(s)/increasing
lp(s)	loop(s)
m	meter(s)
MC	main color
mm	millimeter(s)
oz	ounce(s)
patt(s)	pattern(s); or "work in pattern"
rem	remain(s)/remaining
rep	repeat(s)/repeating
rnd(s)	round(s)
RS	right side
sc	single crochet(s)
sl st	slip stitch
sp(s)	space(s)
st(s)	stitch(es)
tch	turning chain
tog	together
tr	treble(s) crochet
WS	wrong side
yd	yard(s)
yo	yarn over (hook)
[ ]	work instructions within brackets as many times as directed
( )	contains additional instruction or further clarification

Symbols

Increasingly, crochet patterns are being conveyed in the form of diagrams made up of a series of symbols. Although it can take a while to become familiar with this method, once mastered a diagram gives an immediate visual impression of what the crochet will look like.

Basic stitches

- • = slip stitch
- o = chain stitch
- + = single crochet
- ⊤ = half double crochet
- ⊤ = double crochet
- ⊥ = treble crochet
- ⊥ = double treble crochet

Shells
Sometimes symbols are grouped into "V" shapes; this indicates a number of stitches that must be worked into the same stitch or space.

- = 3-dc shell (worked into same space)
- = 5-dc shell (worked into a single stitch)

Bobble, cluster, popcorn, and puff stitches
The symbols for these stitches often look similar to the stitch itself.

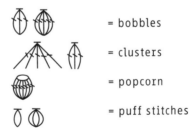

- = bobbles
- = clusters
- = popcorn
- = puff stitches

Other special symbols

- = double around post from front
- = double around post from back
- = dc2tog

stitch
library

basic stitches

Make any number of ch for foundation chain.

Row 1 1 sc in 2nd ch from hook, 1 sc in each of remaining ch to end, turn.
Row 2 Ch 1 (does NOT count as a stitch), 1 sc in each sc to end, turn.
Rep 2nd row to form sc fabric.

Single Crochet

- the most basic stitch, and probably my favorite
- creates a firm, flat fabric
- versatile and reversible
- beautiful for homewares

Make any number of ch for foundation chain.

Row 1 1 hdc in 3rd ch from hook, 1 hdc in each of remaining ch to end, turn.
Row 2 Ch 2 (counts as first hdc), skip first hdc in row below, *1 hdc in next hdc; rep from * to end, work last hdc in top of 2-ch at end, turn.
Rep 2nd row to form hdc fabric.

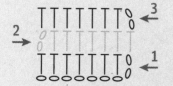

Half Double Crochet

- a basic and satisfying stitch to crochet
- good for when a more fluid fabric is needed
- less compact than single crochet

Double Crochet

- *the fabric grows really quickly with this stitch*
- *great when used in combination with other stitches*

Make any number of ch for foundation chain.

Row 1 1 dc in 4th ch from hook, 1 dc in each of remaining ch to end, turn.
Row 2 Ch 3 (counts as first dc), skip first dc in row below, *1 dc in next dc; rep from * to end, work last dc in top of 3-ch at end, turn.
Rep 2nd row to form dc fabric.

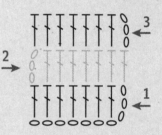

Treble Crochet

- *a very long variation on the basic crochet stitch*
- *a highly decorative stitch*

Make any number of ch for foundation chain.

Row 1 1 tr in 5th ch from hook, 1 tr in each of remaining ch to end, turn.
Row 2 Ch 4 (counts as first tr), skip first tr in row below, *1 tr in next tr; rep from * to end, work last tr in top of 4-ch at end, turn.
Rep 2nd row to form tr fabric.

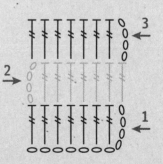

texture stitches

Make an even number of ch for foundation chain.

Row 1 1 sc in 2nd ch from hook, *1 ch, skip 1 ch, 1 sc in next ch; rep from * to end, turn.
Row 2 Ch 1 (does NOT count as a stitch), 1 sc in first sc, 1 sc in next 1-ch sp, *ch 1, 1 sc in next 1-ch sp; rep from * to last sc, 1 sc in last sc, turn.
Row 3 Ch 1 (does NOT count as a stitch), 1 sc in first sc, *ch 1, 1 sc in next 1-ch sp; rep from * to last 2 sc, ch 1, skip 1 sc, 1 sc in last sc, turn.
Rep rows 2 and 3 to form pattern.

Woven Stitch

– one of my favorite stitches
– a lovely discrete texture
– beautifully rustic when worked in a tweed yarn

Make an even number of ch for foundation chain.

Row 1 2 sc in 4th ch from hook, *skip 1 ch, 2 sc in next ch; rep from * to end, turn.
Row 2 Ch 2, skip first sc, 2 sc in next sc, *skip next sc, 2 sc in next sc; rep from * to end, turn.
Rep row 2 to form pattern.

Alternate Stitch

– an easy and pretty stitch
– creates a firm, neat fabric
– made by working two single crochets in every other stitch

Rope Stitch

– *a classic stitch in my books*
– *well suited to baby blankets*
– *the cellular construction of this stitch provides warmth and comfort*

Make a multiple of 3 ch for foundation chain.

Row 1 1 dc in 4th ch from hook, ch 1, 1 dc in next ch, *skip 1 ch, 1 dc in next ch, ch 1, 1 dc in next ch; rep from * to last ch, 1 dc in last ch at end, turn.

Row 2 Ch 3 (counts as first dc), work [1 dc, ch 1, 1 dc] all in each 1-ch sp to end of row, 1 dc in top of 3-ch at end, turn.

Rep row 2 to form pattern.

Note: This stitch is used for the Texture Throw on pages 72–75.

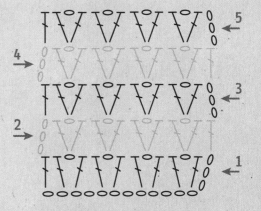

Make a multiple of 8 ch, plus 4 extra, for foundation chain.

Base row (WS) 1 dc in 4th ch from hook, 1 dc in each of remaining ch to end, turn.
Row 1 (RS) Ch 2 (counts as first dc), skip first dc, *[1 dc around post of next dc from front] 4 times, [1 dc around post of next dc from back] 4 times; rep from * to end, 1 dc in top of turning ch at end, turn.
Rows 2, 3, and 4 [Rep 2] 3 times.
Row 5 Ch 2 (counts as first dc), skip first dc, *[1 dc around post of next dc from back] 4 times, [1 dc around post of next dc from front] 4 times; rep from * to end, 1 dc in top of turning ch at end, turn.
Rows 6, 7, and 8 [Rep 5] 3 times.
Rep rows 1–8 to form pattern.

Note: To work "around the post" of a double crochet, wrap the yarn around the hook then insert the hook (from the front or back) through the work between the stitches in the row below and back out again (to the front or back) around the stitch to complete the double.

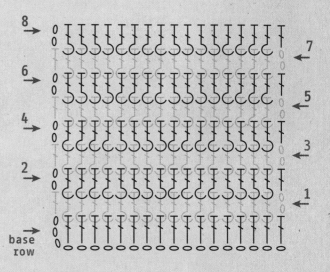

Basketweave Stitch

– *perenially popular stitch*
– *work in really fat yarn to create extreme crochet textures*

clustered and shell stitches

Make a multiple of 2 ch for foundation chain.

1 bobble = [yo and insert hook in st, yo and draw a loop through, yo and draw through first 2 loops on hook] 3 times all in same st, yo and draw a loop through all 4 loops on hook.

Row 1 1 bobble in 4th ch from hook, ch 1, *skip 1 ch, *1 bobble in next ch; rep from * to end, turn.

Row 2 Ch 3, *1 bobble in next 1-ch sp between bobbles of previous row, ch 1; rep from * to end, working last bobble in top of turning chain, turn.
Rep row 2 to form pattern.

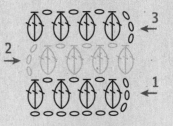

Soft Bobble

- bobbles make attractive round yet flat stitches
- identical on both sides so fully reversible
- perfect for homewares or accessories

Make a multiple of 3 ch for foundation ch.

Row 1 2 dc in 3rd ch from hook, *skip 2 ch, work [1 sc, 2 dc] all in next ch; rep from * to last 3 ch, skip 2 ch, 1 sc in last ch, turn.

Row 2 Ch 2, 2 dc in first sc, *work [1 sc, 2 dc] all in next sc; rep from * to end, 1 sc in turning ch, turn.
Rep row 2 to form pattern.

Ripple Shell Stitch

- a pretty asymmetrical stitch
- rustic yet summery
- particularly lovely when worked in linen

Lace Puff

- *my favorite stitch of all*
- *a soft yarn beautifully enhances this stitch*
- *looks a complex stitch yet is simple to work*

Make a multiple of 6 ch, plus 5 extra, for foundation chain.

1 puff stitch = [yo, insert hook in stitch and draw a long loop through] 4 times in same stitch, yo and draw a loop through all 9 loops on hook.

Row 1 Work [1 dc, ch 2, 1 dc] all in 4th ch from hook, *skip 2 ch, 1 puff stitch in next ch, ch 1 (this chain closes the puff stitch), skip 2 ch, work [1 dc, ch 2, 1 dc] all in next ch; rep from * to last ch, 1 dc in last ch, turn.
Row 2 Ch 3, 1 puff stitch in first 2-ch sp (between 2 dc), ch 1, *work [1 dc, ch 2, 1 dc] all in top of puff stitch (under loop that closes the puff stitch), 1 puff stitch in next 2-ch sp, ch 1; rep from * to end, 1 dc in 3-ch sp at end of row, turn.
Row 3 Ch 3, work [1 dc, ch 2, 1 dc] all in top of first puff stitch, *1 puff stitch in next 2-ch sp, ch 1, work [1 dc, ch 2, 1 dc] all in top of next puff stitch; rep from * to end, 1 dc in 3-ch sp at end of row, turn.
Rep rows 2 and 3 to form pattern.

Note: This stitch is used for the Snood on pages 84–87.

Make a multiple of 10 ch, plus 7 extra, for the foundation chain.

1 cluster = [yo, insert hook in next stitch, yo and draw a loop through, yo and draw through first 2 loops on hook] over the number of sts indicated, yo and draw a loop through all loops on hook to complete cluster.

Row 1 1 sc in 2nd ch from hook, 1 sc in next ch, *skip 3 ch, 7 dc in next ch (these 7 dc in same chain form a 7-dc shell), skip 3 ch, 1 sc in each of next 3 ch; rep from * to last 4 ch, skip 3 ch, 4 dc in last ch, turn.

Row 2 Ch 1, 1 sc in each of first 2 dc, *ch 3, 1 cluster over next 7 sts (that is over next 2 dc, 3 sc, 2 dc), ch 3, 1 sc in each of next 3 dc (these 3 dc are the 3 center sts of the 7-dc shell); rep from * to last 4 sts (remaining 2 dc and 2 sc), finishing with ch 3, 1 cluster over these last 4 sts, turn.

Row 3 Ch 3 (counts as first dc), 3 dc in top of first 4-dc cluster (under loop that closed the cluster), *skip 3-ch sp, 1 sc in each of next 3 sc, skip 3-ch sp, 7 dc in top of next cluster (under loop that closed the cluster); rep from * to last 3-ch sp, finishing with skip 3-ch sp, 1 sc in each of last 2 sc, turn.

Row 4 Ch 3 (counts as first dc), skip first sc, 1 cluster over next 3 sts (that is over next 1 sc, 2 dc), *ch 3, 1 sc in each of next 3 dc (these 3 dc are the 3 center sts of the 7-dc shell), ch 3, 1 cluster over next 7 sts (that is over 2 dc, 3 sc, 2 dc); rep from * to last dc, finishing with ch 3, 1 sc in last dc, 1 sc in top of 3-ch at end of row, turn.

Row 5 Ch 1, 1 sc in each of first 2 sc, *skip 3-ch sp, 7 dc in top of next cluster, skip 3-ch sp, 1 sc in each of next 3 sc; rep from * to last 3-ch sp, finishing with skip 3-ch sp, 4 dc in top of 3-ch at end of row, turn.

Rep rows 2–5 to form pattern.

Note: This reversible stitch is used for the Bolster Cushion on pages 108–11. See page 110 for the stitch diagram.

Catherine Wheel Stitch

– *this stitch creates an exquisite decorative textile*
– *especially interesting when worked in two or even three colors*

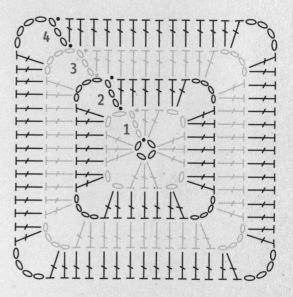

**Double
Crochet Square**

*– a simple, easy-to-master solid-
colored motif*
*– smooth, pared-down texture, good
for understated throws*

Base ring Ch 4 and join with a slip stitch to first chain to form a ring.
Round 1 (RS) Ch 5 (counts as 1 dc and 2-ch sp), [3 dc in ring, ch 2] 3 times, 2 dc in ring, join with a slip stitch to 3rd of 5-ch at beginning of round. *3 dc along each side of square.*
Note: Do not turn at end of rounds but continue with RS of motif always facing.
Round 2 1 slip stitch in first sp, ch 7 (counts as 1 dc and 4-ch sp), 2 dc in same sp, *1 dc in each dc to next sp, work [2 dc, ch 4, 2 dc] all in next sp; rep from * twice more, 1 dc in each dc to next sp, 1 dc in same sp as 7-ch, join with a slip stitch to 3rd of 7-ch at beginning of round. *7 dc along each side of square.*
Round 3 Rep round 2. *11 dc along each side of square.*
Round 4 Rep round 2. *15 dc along each side of square.* Fasten off.

This motif is worked in 3 colors—A, B, and C.

Base ring Using A, ch 6 and join with a slip stitch to first chain to form a ring.

Round 1 (RS) Using A, ch 3 (counts as first dc), 2 dc in ring, [ch 3, 3 dc in ring] 3 times, ch 3, join with a slip stitch to top of 3-ch at beginning of round. Fasten off.

Note: Do not turn at end of rounds but continue with RS of motif always facing.

Round 2 Using B, join yarn with a slip stitch to any 3-ch sp, ch 3 (counts as first dc), [2 dc, ch 3, 3 dc] in same 3-ch sp, *ch 1, [3 dc, ch 3, 3 dc] in next 3-ch sp; rep from * twice more, ch 1, join with a slip stitch to top of 3-ch at beginning of round. Fasten off.

Round 3 Using C, join yarn with a slip stitch to any 3-ch sp, ch 3, [2 dc, ch 3, 3 dc] in same 3-ch sp, *ch 1, 3 dc in next 1-ch sp, ch 1, [3 dc, ch 3, 3 dc] in next 3-ch sp; rep from * twice more, ch 1, 3 dc in next 1-ch sp, ch 1, join with a slip stitch to top of 3-ch at beginning of round. Fasten off.

Round 4 Using A, join yarn with a slip stitch to any 3-ch sp, ch 3, [2 dc, ch 3, 3 dc] in same 3-ch sp, *[ch 1, 3 dc in next 1-ch sp] twice, ch 1, [3 dc, ch 3, 3 dc] in next 3-ch sp; rep from * twice more, [ch 1, 3 dc in next 1-ch sp] twice, ch 1, join with a slip stitch to top of 3-ch at beginning. Fasten off.

Note: This motif is used for the center of the Traditional Motif Blanket on pages 112–15, which is worked in cotton. Traditionally the motif is worked in wool and sometimes with 2-chain rather than 3-chain corners.

Traditional Square

- *timeless classic crochet motif*
- *endless colorway possibilities*
- *equally effective when worked in wool or cotton*

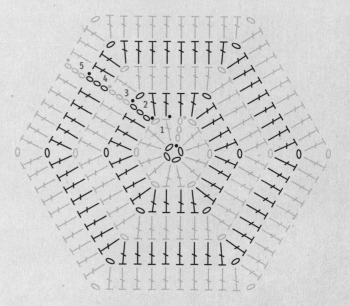

Hexagon

– a lovely motif for patchwork-type throws
– to sharpen the shapes, pin out the finished motifs at the six corners and gently steam

This motif is worked in 2 colors—A and B.

Base ring Using A, ch 4 and join with a slip stitch to first chain to form a ring.

Round 1 (RS) Ch 3 (counts as first dc), 1 dc in ring, [ch 1, 2 dc in ring] 5 times, ch 1, join with a slip stitch to top of 3-ch at beginning of round.

Note: Do not turn at end of rounds but continue with RS of motif always facing.

Round 2 1 slip stitch in first dc, 1 slip stitch in next ch, ch 3 (counts as first dc), *1 dc in each of next 2 dc, work [1 dc, ch 1, 1 dc] in next 1-ch sp; rep from * 4 times more, 1 dc in each of next 2 dc, 1 dc in last 1-ch sp, ch 1, join with a slip stitch to top of 3-ch at beginning of round.

Round 3 Using B, ch 3 (counts as first dc), 1 dc in each dc to first 1-ch sp, work [1 dc, ch 1, 1 dc] in first 1-ch sp, *1 dc in each dc to next 1-ch sp, work [1 dc, ch 1, 1 dc] in next 1-ch sp; rep from * to end, join with a slip stitch to top of 3-ch at beginning of round.

Rounds 4 and 5 [Rep round 3] twice.
Fasten off.

Star Circle

– *worked with ease in only four rounds*
– *attractive star shape at center to show off three contrasting colors*
– *perfect simple shape for coasters*

This motif is worked in 3 colors—A, B, and C.

Base ring Using A, ch 6 and join with a slip stitch to first chain to form a ring.

Round 1 (RS) Ch 4 (counts as first tr), 2 tr in ring, [ch 1, 3 tr in ring] 5 times, ch 1, join with a slip stitch to top of 4-ch at beginning of round, turn.

Round 2 (WS) Ch 1, [1 sc in next 1-ch sp, ch 6] 6 times, join with a slip stitch to first sc. Fasten off.

Round 3 (WS) With WS facing, join B with a slip stitch to a 6-ch sp, ch 2, work [1 hdc, 2 dc, 3 tr, 2 dc, 1 hdc] in each 6-ch sp to end, join with a slip stitch to first hdc, turn. *6 petals.* Fasten off.

Round 4 (RS) With RS facing, join C to first hdc of a petal, ch 4 (counts as first tr), *1 dc in each of next 2 dc, 1 hdc in each of next 3 tr, 1 dc in each of next 2 dc, 1 tr in each of next 2 hdc; rep from * to end, but omitting last tr at end of last repeat, join with a slip stitch to top of 4-ch at beginning of round. Fasten off.

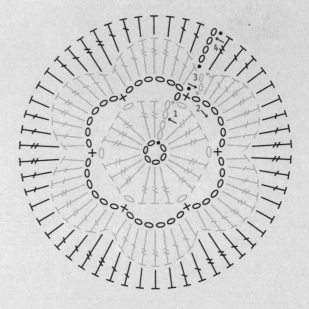

project
workshops

Dishcloth

1

A small yet practical project to get you started with crochet. Making this cloth is the ideal way to practice the basic crochet stitch, single crochet. While the main cloth is worked in single crochet, the contrasting stripes are added to the cloth's surface in slip stitch, a very easy form of crochet embroidery.

Skill level...

BEGINNER

In this project you will learn...
Practicing single crochet
Working slip stitch surface embroidery

Stitches used...
Single crochet; Surface slip stitch

Size
Approximately 10in/25cm wide x 11¾in/30cm long

Materials
Double-knitting weight cotton yarn, such as Rowan Handknit Cotton ③ LIGHT in 2 colors:
  A 2 x 1¾oz/50g balls (93yd/85m per ball) in taupe
  B 1 x 1¾oz/50g ball (93yd/85m per ball) in green
Size H-8 (5mm) crochet hook

Gauge
14 sc and 19 rows to 4in/10cm measured over single crochet using an H-8 (5mm) hook.

Abbreviations
See page 45.

To make dishcloth
Foundation chain Using an H-8 (5mm) hook and A, chain 36.
Row 1 1 sc in 2nd ch from hook, 1 sc in each of remaining ch to end, turn. *35 sc.*

Row 2 Ch 1 (does NOT count as a stitch), 1 sc in each sc to end, turn. *35 sc.*
Repeat row 2 until work measures 11¾in/30cm (approximately 56 rows).
Fasten off.

To finish
Weave in any loose ends.
Lay work out flat and gently steam on wrong side.

Masterclass

Adding surface stripes
First stripe Work the first stripe in surface slip stitches between the 2nd and 3rd rows from the bottom edge of the dishcloth as follows: Using an H-8 (5mm) hook and B, make a slip knot. Remove the hook from slip knot, then insert hook through the dishcloth from the right side of your work one stitch in from the edge, pick up the slip knot again and pull it through to the right side. Keeping the yarn at the wrong side of your work, continue as follows—*insert hook through dishcloth between next 2 stitches, yarn over hook at back of work and pull yarn through dishcloth and loop on hook in one movement. Repeat from * across width of dishcloth, finishing one stitch in from the edge. Fasten off.
Second stripe Work as for the first stripe, but between the 3rd and 4th rows from the top edge of the dishcloth.
Third stripe Work as for the first stripe, but between the 5th and 6th rows from the top edge of the dishcloth.

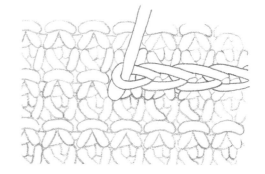

Stripe pillows

A simple square pillow cover made in single and double crochet and worked in varying widths of stripes and colors. The back is soft corduroy fabric but could be worked in crochet, too.

Skill level

BEGINNER

In this project you will learn
Practicing single and double crochet
Working single crochet into the tops of double crochet stitches
Working double crochet stitches into the tops of single crochet stitches
Joining in new colors for stripes, see masterclass on page 67

Stitches used
Single crochet; Double crochet

Size
Size of finished pillow
Approximately 16in/40cm square
Actual size of crocheted pillow front
Approximately 16in/40cm x 16in/40cm

Materials
Stripe 1 pillow (mostly neutral stripe)
A double-knitting-weight linen yarn, such as Rowan Lenpur Linen or any other standard DK yarn (3) LIGHT in 6 colors:
  A 1 x 1³/₄oz/50g ball (125yd/115m per ball) in dark brown
  B 1 x 1³/₄oz/50g ball (125yd/115m per ball) in ecru
  C 1 x 1³/₄oz/50g ball (125yd/115m per ball) in taupe
  D 1 x 1³/₄oz/50g ball (125yd/115m per ball) in light beige
  E 1 x 1³/₄oz/50g ball (125yd/115m per ball) in lime green
  F 1 x 1³/₄oz/50g ball (125yd/115m per ball) in bright pink

Stripe 2 pillow (all color stripe)
Double-knitting-weight linen yarn, such as Rowan Lenpur Linen or any other standard DK yarn (3) LIGHT in 9 colors:
  A 1 x 1³/₄oz/50g ball (125yd/115m per ball) in dark brown
  B 1 x 1³/₄oz/50g ball (125yd/115m per ball) in ecru
  C 1 x 1³/₄oz/50g ball (125yd/115m per ball) in taupe
  D 1 x 1³/₄oz/50g ball (125yd/115m per ball) in light beige
  E 1 x 1³/₄oz/50g ball (125yd/115m per ball) in lime green
  F 1 x 1³/₄oz/50g ball (125yd/115m per ball) in bright pink
  G 1 x 1³/₄oz/50g ball (125yd/115m per ball) in purple
  H 1 x 1³/₄oz/50g ball (125yd/115m per ball) in green
  J 1 x 1³/₄oz/50g ball (125yd/115m per ball) in turquoise

Both pillows
Size E-4 (3.5mm) crochet hook
17in/43cm square of fabric for back of pillow, such as lightweight corduroy or linen, and matching sewing thread
Feather pillow form to fit finished pillow cover

Gauge
17 stitches and 10 rows to 4in/10cm measured over double crochet using an E-4 (3.5mm) hook.

Abbreviations
See page 45.

Special pattern note
Pay careful attention to how to work single crochet into a row of double crochet stitches (as in row 5 of the Stripe 1 Pillow or row 3 of the Stripe 2 Pillow) and also how to work double crochet into a row of single crochet stitches (as in row 7 of the Stripe 1 Pillow or row 4 of the Stripe 2 Pillow). One chain is worked at the beginning of each row of single crochet but this does NOT count as a stitch; three chains are

worked at the beginning of each row of double crochet and this DOES count as a stitch. Count your stitches frequently to make sure you always have 68 stitches in each row.

To make Stripe 1 pillow front

Foundation chain Using an E-4 (3.5mm) hook and A, ch 70.
Row 1 1 dc in 4th ch from hook, 1 dc in each of remaining ch to end, turn. *68 sts.*
Row 2 Ch 3 (counts as first dc), skip first dc in row below, *1 dc in next dc; rep from * to end, then work last dc in top of 3-ch at end, turn.
Rows 3 and 4 Using B, [repeat row 2] twice.
Row 5 Using B, ch 1 (does NOT count as a stitch), 1 sc in each dc to end, then work last sc in top of 3-ch at end, turn. *68 sts.*
Row 6 Using C, ch 1 (does NOT count as a stitch), 1 sc in each sc to end, turn.
Row 7 Using B, ch 3 (counts as first dc), skip first sc in row below, *1 dc in next sc; rep from * to end, turn. *68 sts.*
Row 8 Using C, work in sc (when working sc into a dc row, work as row 5).
Row 9 Using D, work in dc (when working dc into an sc row, work as row 7).
Row 10 Using C, work in sc (as row 5).
Rows 11, 12, and 13 Using D, work in dc.
Row 14 Using D, work in sc.
Rows 15, 16, and 17 Using A, work in dc.
Rows 18 and 19 Using D, work in dc.

Row 20 Using B, work in sc.
Row 21 Using B, work in dc.
Row 22 Using D, work in dc.
Rows 23, 24, 25, and 26 Using C, work in dc.
Row 27 Using C, work in sc.
Row 28 Using E, work in sc.
Row 29 Using E, work in dc.
Row 30 Using C, work in sc.
Row 31 Using A, work in dc.
Row 32 Using A, work in sc.
Rows 33, 34, and 35 Using C, work in dc.
Row 36 Using B, work in dc.
Rows 37 and 38 Using D, work in dc.
Row 39 Using F, work in dc.
Rows 40 and 41 Using D, work in dc.
Row 42 Using C, work in dc.
Rows 43 and 44 Using D, work in dc.
Row 45 Using C, work in sc.
Rows 46 and 47 Using D, work in dc.
Fasten off.

To make Stripe 2 pillow front

Foundation chain Using an E-4 (3.5mm) hook and B, ch 70.
Row 1 1 dc in 4th ch from hook, 1 dc in each of remaining ch to end, turn. *68 sts.*
Row 2 Using G, ch 3 (counts as first dc), skip first dc in row below, *1 dc in next dc; rep from * to end, then work last dc in top of 3-ch at end, turn.
Row 3 Using G, ch 1 (does NOT count as a stitch), 1 sc in each dc to end, then work last sc in top of 3-ch at end, turn. *68 sts.*
Row 4 Using D, ch 3 (counts as first dc), skip first sc in row below, *1 dc in next sc; rep from * to end, turn. *68 sts.*
Row 5 Using D, work in sc (when working sc into a dc row, work as row 3).
Row 6 Using H, work in dc (when working dc into an sc row, work as row 4).
Row 7 Using B, work in dc.
Row 8 Using B, work in sc.
Row 9 Using A, work in dc.
Row 10 Using A, work in sc.
Row 11 Using B, work in dc.
Rows 12 and 13 Using F, work in dc.
Row 14 Using B, work in sc.
Row 15 Using C, work in dc.
Rows 16 and 17 Using B, work in dc.
Row 18 Using J, work in dc.
Rows 19 and 20 Using E, work in dc.
Row 21 Using E, work in sc.

Rows 22 and 23 Using C, work in dc.
Row 24 Using B, work in dc.
Row 25 Using G, work in dc.
Row 26 Using D, work in dc.
Row 27 Using G, work in dc.
Row 28 Using A, work in dc.
Row 29 Using A, work in sc.
Row 30 Using F, work in dc.
Row 31 Using F, work in sc.
Row 32 Using B, work in dc.
Row 33 Using H, work in sc.
Row 34 Using H, work in dc.
Row 35 Using D, work in dc.
Row 36 Using A, work in dc.
Row 37 Using A, work in sc.
Rows 38 and 39 Using B, work in dc.
Row 40 Using J, work in dc.
Rows 41 and 42 Using G, work in dc.

Row 43 Using G, work in sc.
Row 44 Using D, work in dc.
Rows 45 and 46 Using E, work in dc.
Row 47 Using D, work in dc.
Fasten off.

To finish pillow
Weave in any loose ends.
Lay work out flat and gently steam on wrong side.
Fabric pillow back
Press 1/2in/1.5cm to wrong side all around edge of fabric piece for pillow back, so it is same size as crocheted front. Then baste this hem in place. Pin crochet piece to wrong side of fabric, easing to fit if necessary. Baste in place through all layers around three sides. Using sewing thread, sew fabric back to front, leaving one side open. Remove basting.

Masterclass

Joining in new colors

You can work narrow stripes without breaking off the yarn when you change from one color to another. This means that you have less yarn ends to sew in once you have finished the piece. In order to do this, the stripes have to consist of an even number of rows so you are always beginning and ending a color on the same side of the work.

1 In the row before the new stripe color is to be joined in, work to the last stitch, then work the last stitch up to the point when there is one more "yo" left to complete the stitch.

2 Drop the working yarn and wrap the new yarn over the hook and draw it through the remaining loops to complete the stitch.

3 Continue working the turning chain and the subsequent row in the new color. Leave a long enough tail so you can thread the yarn onto a blunt-ended needle and weave it in when you have finished the piece.

Laptop cover

This simple cover for a 13in-/33cm-wide laptop is worked in robust parcel string using single crochet and introduces the techniques of increasing and decreasing. It is finished with a brightly colored zipper.

Skill level

EASY

In this project you will learn
Practicing single crochet
Working with unusual yarn textures
Increasing
Decreasing
Working a single crochet seam

Stitches used
Single crochet

Size
Approximately 13³/4in/35cm x 10in/25.5cm

Materials
A medium-weight soft cotton No. 4 parcel string
(4) MEDIUM in one color:
  4 x 8oz/250g balls (99yd/90m per ball) in ecru
Sizes D-3 (3mm) and E-4 (3.5mm) crochet hooks
20in/50cm bright pink plastic zipper and
  matching sewing thread

Gauge
17¹/2 stitches and 21 rows to 4in/10cm measured over single crochet using an E-4 (3.5mm) hook.

Abbreviations
See page 45.

To make cover front
Foundation chain Using an E-4 (3.5mm) hook and string, ch 50.
Row 1 1 sc in 2nd ch from hook, 1 sc in each of remaining ch to end, turn. *49 sts.*
Row 2 (inc row) Ch 1 (does NOT count as a stitch), 2 sc in first sc, 1 sc in each sc to last sc, 2 sc in last sc, turn. *51 sts. (2 sts increased—one at each end of row.)*
[Repeat row 2] 5 times more. *61 sts.*
Next row Ch 1 (does NOT count as a stitch), 1 sc in each sc to end, turn.
Repeat last row until work measures 8³/4in/22cm from beginning.
Next row (dec row) Ch 1 (does NOT count as a stitch), insert hook in first sc, yo and draw a loop through, insert hook in next sc, yo and draw a loop through, yo and draw through all 3 loops on hook, 1 sc in each sc to last 2 sc, [insert hook in next sc, yo and draw a loop through] twice, yo and draw through all 3 loops on hook, turn. *59 sts. (2 sts decreased—one at each end of row.)*
Repeat last row 5 times more. *49 sts.*
Next row Ch 1 (does NOT count as a stitch), 1 sc in each sc to end.
Fasten off.

To make cover back
Make exactly as for front.

To finish
Weave in any loose ends.
Lay work out flat and gently steam on wrong side.

Single crochet seam
Place the the front piece on top of the back piece. Then using a D-3 (3mm) hook and string, work sc evenly along the edge through both layers, leaving a 20in/50cm opening at one end of the case. (This seam remains on the outside of the case.)

Zipper opening
The zipper is sewn to the outside of the case to form a decorative border along the outer edge of the opening on the front and back of the case. To do this, fold the zipper in half lengthwise with wrong sides together, then position the wrong side of one zipper tape on the right side of the front of the case along the opening, and the wrong side of the other zipper tape on the right side of the back of the case. Pin, then baste the zipper in place. Sew the zipper tape to the case along the outer edge of both zipper tapes, using small overcast stitches. Remove the basting.

Masterclass

Increasing at the start of the row

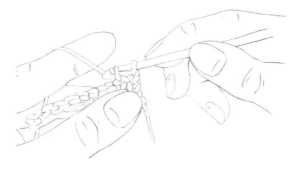

1 Make a turning chain of the appropriate height—the laptop cover is worked in single crochet, so here it is one chain. Work a single crochet into the first stitch.

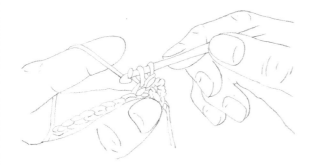

2 Work another single crochet into the same stitch to increase by one stitch. Continue to the end of the row. (For a smoother edge, you can work the extra stitch into the second stitch instead of the first.)

Increasing at the end of the row

1 Work to the last stitch in the row and work a single crochet into this stitch.

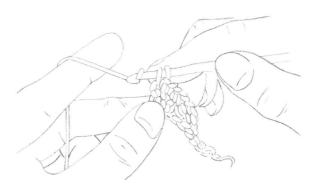

2 Work another single crochet into the same stitch to increase by one stitch. (For a smoother edge, work the extra stitch into the second to last stitch instead of the last.)

Texture throw

I loved the blankets that were always folded on the bottom of the bed at my granny's, just in case it got chilly in the night. Inspired by that memory, I have given this simple throw a more contemporary look worked in British sheep breeds wool in a natural, neutral color. The bulky-weight yarn gives an authentic country—but more luxurious—take on this classic. It is crocheted in easy rope stitch with a half-double border, which gives a lovely contrast.

Skill level

■■□□□
EASY

In this project you will learn
A new stitch, called rope stitch
Working on a large scale
Adding an edging
Practicing half double crochet

Stitches used
Rope stitch, using double crochet and chains
Half double crochet

Size
Approximately 53½in/134cm x 61½in/154cm

Materials
A bulky-weight wool yarn, such as Rowan Purelife British Sheep Breeds Chunky Undyed 🔵5 BULKY in one color:
   16 x 3½oz/100g balls (120yd/110m per ball) in light gray
Sizes K-10½ (7mm) and L-11 (8mm) crochet hooks

Gauge
3½ V-stitches and 5 rows to 4in/10cm measured over rope stitch pattern using an L-11 (8mm) hook. 10½ hdc and 9 rows to 4in/10cm measured over simple hdc edging stitch pattern using a K-10½ (7mm) hook.

Abbreviations
See page 45.

Special pattern note
To work a gauge swatch in rope stitch, make a multiple of 3 chains for the foundation chain—18 chains will be sufficient. Using an L-11 (8mm) hook, work rows 1 and 2 of the pattern, then repeat row 2 until the swatch measures approximately 5in/13cm long. This will create a swatch big enough to test your gauge.

To make throw
Foundation chain Using an L-11 (8mm) hook, ch 129.
Begin the rope stitch pattern as follows:
Row 1 1 dc in 4th chain from hook, ch 1, 1 dc in next ch, *skip 1 ch, 1 dc in next ch, ch 1, 1 dc in next ch; rep from * to last ch, 1 dc in last ch at end, turn.
Row 2 Ch 3, work [1 dc, ch 1, 1 dc] all in each 1-ch sp to end of row, 1 dc in top of 3-ch at end, turn. *42-V stitches.*
Repeat row 2 to form the rope stitch pattern and continue in rope stitch until work measures 56in/140cm from beginning (approximately 70 rows in total).
Fasten off.

To finish
The simple hdc edging stitch is worked in rounds all around the outside edge of the throw.

Edging

Using a K-10½ (7mm) hook, join yarn to edge of throw with a slip stitch by inserting hook through a chain near the center of the foundation-chain edge of the throw and drawing a loop through, then work the border in rounds as follows:

Round 1 Ch 2, 1 hdc in same place as slip stitch, 1 hdc in next ch, then continue in hdc around throw, working 1 hdc in each foundation chain, 2 hdc in each row end along the sides (into either the space below the dc or the space formed by the 3-ch turning chain), 1 hdc in each stitch across the last row and 3 hdc in each corner, join with a slip stitch to top of first hdc.

Note: Do not turn at end of rounds but continue with the same side of throw always facing.

Round 2 Ch 2, 1 hdc in same place as slip stitch, then continue in hdc around throw, working 1 hdc in each hdc and 3 hdc in center hdc of each 3-hdc group at each of 4 corners, join with a slip stitch to top of first hdc of round.

Rounds 3, 4, 5, and 6 [Repeat round 2] 4 times more—border measures approximately 2¾in/7cm. Fasten off.

Weave in any loose ends.

Stitch diagram Rope Stitch

KEY

O = chain stitch

T = double crochet

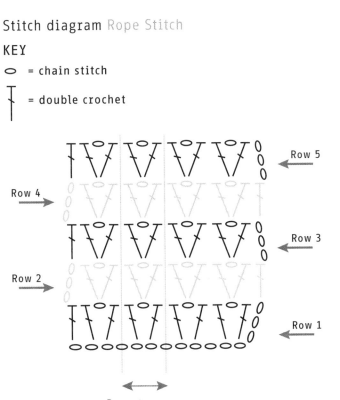

Row 5

Row 4

Row 3

Row 2

Row 1

Repeat as many times as necessary

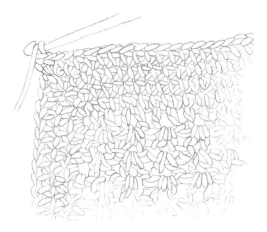

Contemporary clutch

A crocheted strip, consisting of a combination of double crochet bobbles and shells, forms the decorative fabric of this simple clutch bag. Fastened with a plain zipper, the straight lines enhance the contemporary feel of this fold-over bag, but also makes it the perfect practice piece as no shaping is required. The vibrant orange lining creates a contrasting backdrop for the neutral yarn, which beautifully showcases the "thistle pattern."

Skill level

▰▰▱▱ **EASY**

In this project you will learn
Making bobbles
Working shells

Stitches used
Double crochet
Double crochet bobbles
Double crochet shells

Size
Approximately 10in/25cm wide x 6–6³/₄in/15–17cm deep when folded

Materials
Aran-weight cotton-and-silk mix yarn, such as Rowan Savannah **④** MEDIUM in one color:
  4 x 1³/₄oz/50g balls (87yd/80m per ball) in beige
Size J-10 (6mm) crochet hook
10in/25cm contrasting zipper and matching sewing thread
¹/₂yd/0.5m lining fabric in same color as zipper

Gauge
3 shells and 5 rows to 4in/10cm measured over thistle pattern using a J-10 (6mm) hook and yarn double.

Abbreviations
1 bobble = [yo and insert hook in next st, yo and draw a loop through, yo and draw through first 2 loops on hook] 3 times all in same st, yo and draw a loop through all 4 loops on hook.
See also page 45.

Special notes
Use two strands of yarn held together throughout. To work a gauge swatch in the thistle pattern, make a multiple of 4 chains, plus 3 chains extra, for the foundation chain—19 chains will be sufficient. Using a J-10 (6mm) hook and two strands of yarn held together, work rows 1–3 of the pattern, then repeat rows 2 and 3 until the swatch measures approximately 5in/13cm long. This will create a swatch big enough to test your gauge.

To finish

Weave in any loose ends.
Lay work out flat and gently steam on wrong side.
Cut lining fabric to same size as crochet piece, but allowing 1/2in/1.5cm extra all around for hem. Fold under hem along edges of lining and pin to wrong side of crochet so fold is about 1/4in/5mm from the edge of the piece along all four sides. Using matching sewing thread, stitch lining in place.
Fold piece in half widthwise with right sides together and stitch side seams, using yarn.
Turn bag right side out and sew zipper across the opening to right side of bag, using matching sewing thread. Fold bag in half again.

To make bag

Foundation chain Using a J-10 (6mm) hook and yarn double, ch 31.
Row 1 (RS) 1 dcr in 4th ch from hook, 1 dc in each of next 2 ch, *ch 2, skip 1 ch, 1 dc in each of next 3 ch; rep from * to last ch, 1 dc in last ch, turn.
Row 2 Ch 3 (counts as first dc), skip first 2 dc, work [1 bobble, ch 3, 1 bobble] all in next dc, *skip next [1 dc, 2-ch sp, 1 dc], work [1 bobble, ch 3, 1 bobble] all in next dc; rep from * to last dc, skip last dc and work 1 dc in top of 3-ch at end, turn.
Row 3 Ch 3, 3 dc in first 3-ch arch (these 3 dc form the first 3-dc shell), *ch 2, 3 dc in next 3-ch arch; rep from * to end, 1 dc in top of 3-ch at end, turn.
Repeat rows 2 and 3 to form thistle pattern and continue in pattern until work measures 23³/4in/60cm.
Fasten off.

Stitch diagram Thistle Pattern

KEY

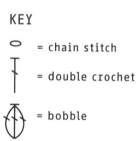

o = chain stitch

⊤ = double crochet

= bobble

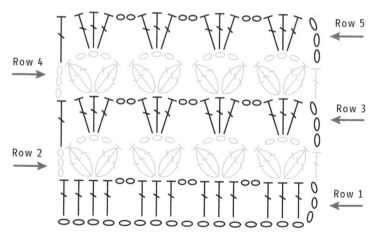

Row 5

Row 4

Row 3

Row 2

Row 1

Masterclass

Working a double crochet bobble
A bobble is created by a raised cluster of stitches that sit on the surface of the crochet. All the stitches that make up the bobble are worked up to their last loop into the same place and then pulled together with a chain at the top of the stitch.

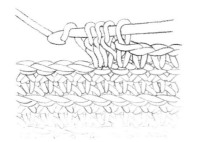

1 With the wrong side facing, work to where a bobble is required. Work 3 incomplete double crochets, leaving the last loop of each stitch on the hook, so 4 loops remain.

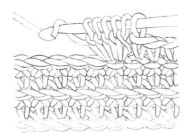

2 Work 2 more incomplete double crochets, to leave 6 loops on the hook. Wrap the yarn over the hook and draw through all the loops on the hook.

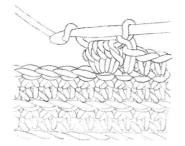

3 Wrap the yarn over the hook one last time and draw through the loop on the hook. Gently push the group of stitches through to the right side of the work.

Working a double crochet shell
A shell, or a fan, is usually made up of several of the same type of stitch worked into one place to create a shell-like effect. Usually all the constituent stitches of the shell are worked into a single stitch, rather than a chain space. This helps to hold the base of the shell together, leaving the upper ends of the stitches to fan out.

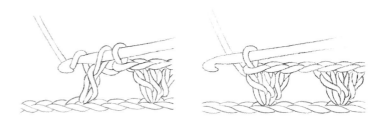

1 Work to where the shell is required, skip the number of chains/stitches specified in the pattern (here skip 3 chain). Work a stitch into the next chain/stitch.

2 Work another 2 stitches into the same chain/stitch, thus completing one shell.

Working a double crochet half shell at the end of a row

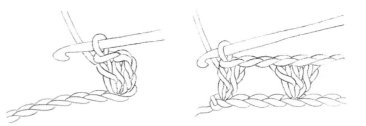

3 In order to keep the stitch count correct it may be necessary to work a half shell at the beginning or end of the row. To do this at the beginning of the row, work 2 stitches into the first stitch.

4 To do this at the end of the row, work 2 stitches into the final stitch of the row.

Fingerless mittens

Fashionably stylish and practical
fingerless mittens worked in a
decorative crochet stitch in cozy
baby alpaca yarn. The thumb holes
are created simply by skipping a few
stitches in a row, that's all.

Skill level

INTERMEDIATE

In this project you will learn
Practicing half double crochet
Working a horizontal thumb hole
Working pattern repeats

Stitches used
Half double crochet; Double crochet
Double crochet bobbles

Size
One size to fit average-size woman's hand—
finished length 15in/38cm

Materials
Light double-knitting-weight alpaca yarn, such as
Rowan Baby Alpaca DK ❨3❩ LIGHT in one color:
   4 x 1¾oz/50g balls (109yd/100m per ball)
   in light gray
Sizes E-4 (3.5mm) and G-6 (4mm) crochet hooks

Gauge
8 bobbles and 11 rows to 4in/10cm measured over
zigzag lozenge stitch using a G-6 (4mm) hook.

Abbreviations
1 bobble = [yo and insert hook in 1-ch sp, yo and
draw a loop through, yo and draw through first 2
loops on hook] 3 times all in same 1-ch sp, yo and
draw a loop through all 4 loops on hook.
1 half bobble = [yo and insert hook in 1-ch sp,
yo and draw a loop through, yo and draw through
first 2 loops on hook] twice all in same 1-ch sp,
yo and draw a loop through all 3 loops on hook.
See also page 45.

To make mittens
Foundation chain Using a G-6 (4mm) hook, ch 37
loosely.
Work a border of 2 rows of half double crochet as
follows:
Row 1 1 hdc in 3rd ch from hook, 1 hdc in each of
remaining ch to end, turn.
Row 2 Ch 2 (counts as first hdc), skip first hdc,
*1 hdc in next hdc; rep from * to end, then work
last hdc in top of 2-ch at end, turn. *36 sts.*
Continue in zigzag lozenge stitch as follows:
Patt row 1 (WS) Ch 2 (counts as first hdc), 1 hdc
in first hdc, *skip 1 hdc, work [1 hdc, ch 1, 1 hdc]
all in next hdc; rep from * to last 2 hdc, skip 1
hdc, 2 hdc in last hdc, turn.
Patt row 2 (RS) Ch 3, 1 dc in first hdc (counts as
a half bobble), *ch 1, 1 bobble in next 1-ch sp;
rep from * to end, ch 1, 1 half bobble in top of
2-ch at end of row, turn. *16 bobbles and 2 half
bobbles.*
Patt row 3 Ch 2 (counts as first hdc), *work [1
hdc, ch 1, 1 hdc] all in next 1-ch sp; rep from *
to end, 1 hdc in top of 3-ch at end of row, turn.
Patt row 4 Ch 3 (counts as first dc), *1 bobble
in next 1-ch sp, ch 1; rep from * to last 1-ch sp,
1 bobble in last sp, 1 dc in top of 2-ch at end of
row, turn. *17 bobbles.*
Patt row 5 Ch 2 (counts as first hdc), 1 hdc in
first dc, *work [1 hdc, ch 1, 1 hdc] all in next 1-ch
sp; rep from * to end, 2 hdc in top of 3-ch at end
of row, turn.
[Repeat patt rows 2–5] 4 times more.
Change to an E-4 hook and [repeat patt rows 2–5]
3 times more, so ending with a WS row.
Mitten should now measure approximately
12¾in/32cm from beginning.

Masterclass

Working a horizontal thumb hole or buttonhole

The simplest way to work an opening, whether it is for a thumb hole or buttonhole, is to skip a number of stitches in a row. At the position at which the hole is required, work a number of chain stitches that will accommodate the thumb or the diameter of the button (for these mittens, work 6 chain). Skip the number of stitches for which you have worked chain, then continue in the pattern. On the next row, work over the chain, making the same number of stitches as there are chain.

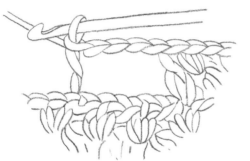

Work thumb hole

Next row (RS) Ch 3, 1 dc in first hdc, *ch 1, 1 bobble in next 1-ch sp; rep from * 6 times more; ch 6, skip next 2 1-ch sps, 1 bobble in next ch sp, **ch 1, 1 bobble in next ch sp; rep from ** to end, ch 1, 1 half bobble in top of 2-ch at end of row, turn.
Next row Ch 2, *work [1 hdc, ch 1, 1 hdc] all in next 1-ch sp; rep from * 6 times more; [1 hdc, ch 1, 1 hdc] twice in 6-ch sp, **work [1 hdc, ch 1, 1 hdc] all in next 1-ch sp; rep from ** to end, 1 hdc in top of 3-ch at end of row, turn.
Next row Rep patt row 4. *16 bobbles.*
Next row Rep patt row 5.
Next row Rep patt row 2. *15 bobbles and 2 half bobbles.*
Next row Rep patt row 3. Fasten off.
Work second mitten in exactly the same way.

To finish

Weave in any loose ends. Gently steam on wrong side. Sew side seams.

Stitch diagrams Zigzag Lozenge Stitch

KEY

○ = chain stitch
T = half double crochet
𝖳 = double crochet
◊ = bobble
◊ = half bobble

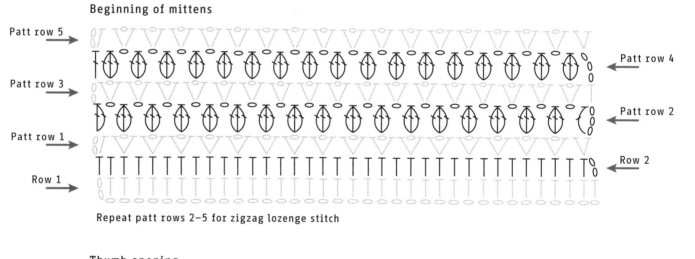

Beginning of mittens

Patt row 5
Patt row 3
Patt row 1
Row 1

Patt row 4
Patt row 2
Row 2

Repeat patt rows 2–5 for zigzag lozenge stitch

Thumb opening

Classic snood

7

A simple, luxurious and now classic snood designed to be worn around the neck in two or three loops. Worked in lace clusters, this crocheted textile has a bubbly texture of thick puffs combined with openwork V-stitches.

Skill level

◖◼◼◼▭
INTERMEDIATE

In this project you will learn
Practicing double crochet
A new stitch, called puff stitch

Stitches used
Double crochet
Puff stitch

Size
Approximately 10in/25cm x 50in/127cm

Materials
Aran-weight alpaca-mix yarn, such as Rowan Lima
(4) MEDIUM in one color:
   5 x 1¾oz/50g balls (109yd/100m per ball)
   in pale beige
Size H-8 (5mm) crochet hook

Gauge
3 stitch groups (each stitch group is made up of—1 puff stitch, ch 1, 1 dc, ch 2, 1 dc of pattern) and 9 rows to 4in/10cm measured over lace puff stitch using an H-8 (5mm) hook.

Abbreviations
1 puff stitch = [yo, insert hook in stitch and draw a long loop through] 4 times in same stitch, yo and draw a loop through all 9 loops on hook. See also page 45.

Stitch diagram
See page 54 for the symbol diagram for the lace puff stitch.

Special pattern note
To work a gauge swatch in the lace puff stitch, make a multiple of 6 chains, plus 5 chains extra, for the foundation chain—29 chains will be sufficient. Using an H-8 (5mm) hook, work rows 1–3 of the pattern, then repeat rows 2 and 3 until the swatch measures approximately 5in/13cm long. This will create a swatch big enough to test your gauge.

To make snood
Foundation chain Using an H-8 (5mm) hook, ch 47.
Row 1 Work [1 dc, ch 2, 1 dc] all in 4th chain from hook, *skip 2 ch, 1 puff stitch in next ch, ch 1 (this chain closes the puff stitch), skip 2 ch, work [1 dc, ch 2, 1 dc] all in next ch; rep from * to last ch, 1 dc in last ch, turn.
Row 2 Ch 3, 1 puff stitch in first 2-ch sp (between 2 dc), ch 1, *work [1 dc, ch 2, 1 dc] all in top of next puff stitch (under loop that closes the puff stitch), 1 puff stitch in next 2-ch sp, ch 1; rep from * to end, 1 dc in 3-ch sp at end of row, turn.
Row 3 Ch 3, work [1 dc, ch 2, 1 dc] all in top of first puff stitch, *1 puff stitch in next 2-ch sp, ch 1, work [1 dc, ch 2, 1 dc] all in top of next puff stitch; rep from * to end, 1 dc in 3-ch sp at end of row, turn.
Repeat rows 2 and 3 to form the lace puff stitch and continue in pattern until work measures 50in/127cm.
Fasten off.

To finish
Weave in any loose ends.
Twist the snood once in the middle of the length and sew the ends together.

Masterclass

The stitch pattern used to great decorative effect in this snood is made by working a combination of puff stitches and openwork V-stitches.

Working puff stitch

There are various ways of working puff stitches but they all add raised texture to otherwise flat surfaces.

1 Work 3 chain, then wrap the yarn over the hook.

2 Insert the hook into the next stitch and draw the loop through.

3 Repeat this three more times so there are nine loops on the hook.

4 Wrap the yarn over the hook and draw through all nine loops on the hook. Work one chain to close and complete the puff stitch.

Working openwork V-stitches

5 Work 1 double into the top of the completed puff stitch in the row below, then work 2 chain.

6 Work a further 1 double crochet into the top of the same puff stitch.

7 Continue working alternate puff stitches and V-stitches to the last puff stitch in the row.

8 Work 1 double into the turning-chain space, turn.

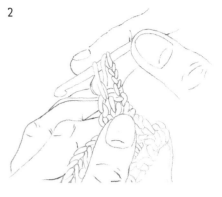

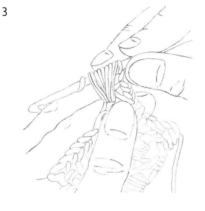

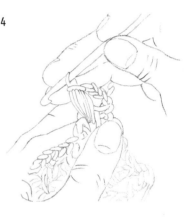

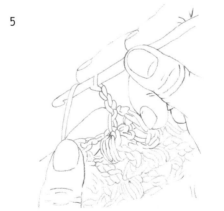

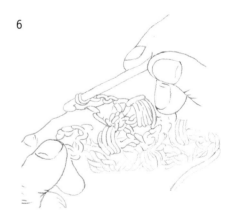

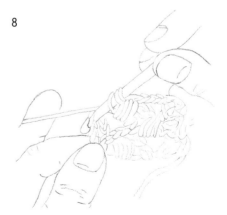

Triangular scarf

The intricate appearance of the lace stitches that make up this elegant scarf belies the simplicity of the pattern. With incremental decreases worked block by block, the scarf takes on a gently stepped triangular shape. I have used a very fine laceweight yarn in a deep plum shade to complement the filigree openwork stitches.

Skill level

INTERMEDIATE

In this project you will learn
Decreasing on a stitch pattern to form a triangle
Working with a laceweight yarn

Stitches used
Single crochet
Double crochet

Size
Approximately 61in/154cm across the widest part x 31¼in/79cm from center of foundation-chain edge to tip of triangle

Materials
Lace-weight alpaca and wool yarn, such as Rowan Fine Lace 🔘 LACE in one color:
  2 x 1¾oz/50g balls (437yd/400m per ball) in deep plum
Sizes G-6 (4mm) and H-8 (5mm) crochet hooks

Gauge
3½ stitch repeats and 16 rows to 4in/10cm measured over pattern using a G-6 (4mm) hook.

Abbreviations
See page 45.

Special note
The starburst pattern is worked over a multiple of 6 foundation chains, plus 3 extra. If you are changing the size of the triangle, be sure to start with an odd number of stitch repeats (an odd number of 6-chain groups) so that at the finish of the decreasing you are left with one repeat at the center.

To make scarf triangle
The scarf is begun along the longest edge and decreased gradually at each side edge to form a triangle.
Foundation chain Using an H-8 hook, ch 285 loosely.
Change to a G-6 (4mm) hook and continue in starburst pattern as follows:
Row 1 (RS) 1 sc in 2nd ch from hook, 1 sc in next ch, *ch 6, skip 4 ch, 1 sc in each of next 2 ch; rep from * to end, turn.
Row 2 Ch 3 (counts as first dc), skip first sc, 1 dc in next sc, *ch 2, 1 sc in 6-ch arch, ch 2, 1 dc in each of next 2 sc; rep from * to end, turn.
Row 3 Ch 3, skip first dc, 1 dc in next dc, *ch 3, 1 slip stitch in next sc, ch 3, 1 dc in each of next 2 dc; rep from * to end, working last dc of last repeat in top of 3-ch at end of row, turn.
Row 4 Ch 1, 1 sc in each of first 2 dc, *ch 4, 1 sc in each of next 2 dc; rep from * to end, working last sc of last repeat in top of 3-ch at end of row, turn.
Row 5 (decrease row) Skip first sc, slip stitch across next sc and 4 ch, ch 1, 1 sc in each of next 2 sc, *ch 6, 1 sc in each of next 2 sc; rep from * until 4-ch and 2 sc remain, turn. *2 stitch repeats decreased.*

Repeat rows 2–5 to form the scarf triangle, decreasing one stitch repeat at each end on every 4th row (every *row 5*) as set, until only one stitch repeat remains to be worked.
Work rows 2–4 as set, then work the last row.
Last row Ch 1, 1 sc in each of first 2 sc, ch 6, 1 sc in each of next 2 sc.
Fasten off.

To finish
Weave in any loose ends.
Edging
With RS of work facing and using a G-6 (4mm) hook, position the starting chain near you and join yarn with a slip stitch to the first slip stitch in the 5th row from the start (on the right edge of the scarf), then work edging as follows:
Round 1 *Ch 4, 1 dc in inner corner formed by decrease, ch 4, 1 slip stitch in outer corner of next block*; rep from * to * point of the scarf, ch 4, 1 dc in 6-ch sp at point, ch 4, 1 slip stitch to outer corner of same block, then rep from * to * along other edge of scarf. Fasten off.
Lay scarf out flat and steam gently on wrong side.

Stitch diagram Starburst Pattern

KEY
- • = slip stitch
- o = chain stitch
- + = single crochet
- ⊤ = double crochet

Traditionally crochet sought to imitate beautiful Flemish lace and initially was worked using extremely fine yarns, most especially linen or cotton. Often one can only stare in wonderment at the intricate finesse of vintage crochet pieces.

Working with laceweight yarns can seem intimidating as they appear slow and tedious to work with. However, working with extremely fine yarns allows endless creative possibilities. I most especially like to crochet relatively traditional openwork stitches but with a large hook. The resulting textile is unexpected, interesting, and gives a beautiful new perspective to a garment.

Gossamer-fine shawls, wraps, and scarves are lovely to work in this experimental way and, moreover, they work up quickly when made with a large, rather than tiny, hook. Furthermore, laceweight yarn has great yardage so it really does go a long, long way, making those exquisite hand-dyed laceweight yarns, which are increasingly available, look a little more justifiable in price.

Generally when crocheting with ultra-fine yarns —or whisper-fine, as I like to call them—I work the foundation row loosely by going up a hook size so that it creates more flexibity.

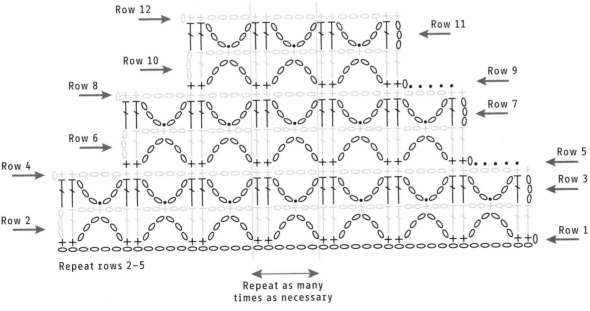

Repeat rows 2–5

Repeat as many times as necessary

Slipper boots

Crocheted in firm, dense single crochet using a robust, hardwearing British sheeps breed wool, this is my take on the ubiquitous twenty-first century footwear: the slipper boot.

Skill level

INTERMEDIATE

In this project you will learn
Working a simple single crochet decrease
Working a simple single crochet increase
Designing to fit your size

Stitches used
Single crochet

Size
Sole of this woman's slipper measures approximately 9¹/₂in/24.5cm long (to adjust size, see masterclass on page 94)

Materials
Bulky-weight wool yarn, such as Rowan Purelife British Sheep Breeds Chunky Undyed (5) BULKY in one color:
  2 x 3¹/₂oz/100g balls (120yd/110m per ball) in light gray
K-10¹/₂ (7mm) crochet hook
Scraps of leather, or suede, and matching sewing thread

Gauge
10 sts and 14 rows to 4in/10cm measured over single crochet using a K-10¹/₂ (7mm) hook.

Abbreviations
sc2tog = [insert hook in next st, yo and draw a loop through] twice, yo and draw through all 3 loops on hook—one stitch decreased.
See also page 45.

To make slipper uppers (make 2)
The slippers are made in two separate pieces—the upper and the sole.
Leg
The leg of the upper is worked in rounds as follows:
Base ring Using a K-10¹/₂ (7mm) hook, ch 31 and join with a slip stitch to first chain to form a ring. (Make sure that the chain is not twisted when you join the chain into a ring.)
Round 1 (WS) Ch 1, 1 sc in same place as slip stitch, 1 sc in each of remaining ch to end, join with a slip stitch to first sc. *31 sc.*
Note: Do not turn at end of rounds but continue with WS always facing.
Round 2 Ch 1, 1 sc in same place as slip stitch, 1 sc in each sc to end, join with a slip stitch to first sc. *31 sc.*
Repeat last round 4 times more.
Heel
The heel is worked in rows as follows:
Row 1 (WS) Ch 1, 1 sc in same place as slip stitch, 1 sc in each sc to end, turn. *31 sc.*
Row 2 (RS) Ch 1, 1 sc in each sc to end, turn.
Row 3 Ch 1, sc2tog, 1 sc in each sc to last 2 sc, sc2tog, turn. *29 sc.*
Row 4 Ch 1, 1 sc in each sc to end, turn.
Row 5 Ch 1, 1 sc in each sc to end, turn.
Instep
The instep is worked in rounds as follows:
Round 6 (RS) Ch 1, 1 sc in each sc to last sc, 2 sc in last sc, then work 11 sc across instep (row-end edges), join with a slip stitch to first sc.
Round 7 Ch 1, 1 sc in same place as slip stitch, 1 sc in each sc to end, join with a slip stitch to first sc, turn.

Top of foot
Starting with a WS row, the foot is worked in rows as follows:
Row 8 Ch 1, 1 sc in each of next 14 sc, turn. *14 sc.*
Rows 9, 10, and 11 [Rep row 8] 3 times.
Row 12 Ch 1, 1 sc in each sc to last 2 sc, sc2tog, turn. *13 sc.*
Row 13 Ch 1, 1 sc in each sc to last 2 sc, sc2tog, turn. *12 dc.*
Rows 14 and 15 Ch 1, 1 sc in each sc to end, turn.
Row 16 Ch 1, 1 sc in each sc to last 2 sc, sc2tog, turn. *11 sc.*
Row 17 Ch 1, 1 sc in each sc to last 2 sc, sc2tog, turn. *10 sc.*
Row 18 Ch 1, 1 sc in each sc to last 2 sc, sc2tog, turn. *9 sc.*
Row 19 Ch 1, 1 sc in each sc to last 2 sc, sc2tog, turn. *8 sc.*
Fasten off and turn leg right side out.
Make second upper in exactly the same way.

To make soles (make 2)
The sole is worked from the heel to the toe.
Foundation chain Using a K-10½ (7mm) hook, ch 5.
Row 1 1 sc in 2nd ch from hook, 1 sc in each of remaining ch to end, turn. *4 sc.*
Row 2 Ch 1, 1 sc in each sc to end, turn.
Row 3 Ch 1, 2 sc in first sc, 1 sc in each sc to last sc, 2 sc in last sc, turn. *6 sc.*
Repeat row 2 until work measures 5¼in/13.5cm from beginning.
Next row Ch 1, 2 sc in first sc, 1 sc in each sc to last sc, 2 sc in last sc, turn. *8 sc.*
Repeat row 2 until work measures 9in/23cm from beginning.
Next row Ch 1, sc2tog, 1 sc in each sc to last 2 sc, sc2tog, turn. *6 sc.*
Next row Ch 1, sc2tog, 1 sc in each sc to last 2 sc, sc2tog, turn. *4 sc.*
Fasten off.
Make second sole in exactly the same way.

To finish
Weave in any loose ends.
Pin sole to upper with wrong sides together, easing to fit around toe. Using a K-10½ (7mm) hook, join yarn with a slip stitch to center of heel, inserting hook through both layers, work ch 1, then work sc through both layers all around, join with a slip stitch to first sc.
Fasten off and weave in end.
If desired, turn down first three rows of leg to form a "cuff" at top of slipper.
Cut two pieces of leather for each slipper, using the two templates (see page 143), one for the sole under the ball of the foot and one for the sole under the heel. Hand sew these leather pads to the soles, using a matching sewing thread.
Note: To make the hand sewing easier, if you have a sewing machine use it to punch holes through the leather. Set the sewing machine to an extra-long stitch and do not thread the needle, then stitch all around the cut out shapes, ⅛in/4mm from the edge. Overcast stitch the pieces in place through the punched holes.

Masterclass

Adjusting the slipper pattern for different sizes
One of crochet's greatest qualitites is its flexibility. As this slipper boot is worked in basic single crochet, it very easy to adjust the length and width of the basic shape to suit different foot sizes. If you have a narrow foot, take out 2 chain from the width of the sole and 2 stitches from the top of the foot; or, alternatively, if you have a wide foot, add 2 chain (and 2 stitches) to the width. Alter the length of the foot by working fewer or more rows within the straight sole (and top of foot) section. As a general tip, add or subtract ½in/1cm if you wish to make a larger or smaller size. This is a very versatile pattern: I prefer a short boot that I wear with the edge rolled down to form a cuff, but you can work a longer cuff for a higher boot and even work the initial row in a contrasting yarn to give a further decorative detail.

Bejeweled brooches

An extremely easy, learn-to-crochet project for practicing and perfecting work in the round. These simple round motifs are worked in jewel-color yarns and embellished with vibrant stones and other gems to create jewelry pins. If you can't find suitable gem stones to buy, break up an inexpensive secondhand piece. I like to wear two or three of these brooches together.

Skill level

BEGINNER

In this project you will learn
Making a simple round motif

Stitches used
Single crochet
Double crochet

Sizes
Small brooch: Approximately 1¹/₂in/3.5cm in diameter
Large brooch: Approximately 1³/₄in/4.5cm in diameter

Materials
Double-knitting-weight linen yarn, such as Rowan Lenpur Linen **(3)** LIGHT or a natural hemp yarn of the same weight, in desired color for each brooch:
    small amounts of 1³/₄oz/50g balls (126yd/115m per ball) in gray, purple, and chartreuse
Size G-6 (4mm) crochet hook
Large square- or round-shaped jewels or crystals with holes, or large decorative buttons
Brooch pin for each brooch
Scrap of leather or felt and matching sewing thread

Gauge
It is not essential to work to a specific gauge for this project.

Abbreviations
See page 45.

Special yarn note
Use two strands of yarn held together throughout.

To make small brooch
Base ring Using a G-6 (4mm) hook and yarn double, ch 3 and join with a slip stitch to first ch to form a ring.
Round 1 (WS) Ch 1, 8 sc in ring, join with a slip stitch to 1-ch at beginning of round.
Note: Do not turn at end of rounds but continue with WS of brooch always facing.
Round 2 Ch 1, [1 sc in next sc, 2 sc in next sc] 4 times, join with a slip stitch to 1-ch at beginning of round.
Round 3 Ch 1, [insert hook through center hole, yo and draw a long loop through, yo and draw a loop through 2 loops on hook] 16 times, join with a slip stitch to 1-ch at beginning of round.
Round 4 Ch 1, [skip next st, 1 sc in next st] 8 times, join with a slip stitch to 1-ch at beginning of round.
Fasten off, leaving a long loose end.

To make large brooch

Base ring Using a G-6 (4mm) hook and yarn double, ch 3 and join with a slip stitch to first ch to form a ring.

Round 1 Ch 1, 8 sc in ring, join with a slip stitch to 1-ch at beginning of round.

Note: Do not turn at end of rounds but continue with same side of brooch always facing.

Round 2 Ch 3, [1 dc in next sc, 2 dc in next sc] 4 times, join with a slip stitch to top of 3-ch at beginning of round.

Round 3 Ch 1, [insert hook through center hole, yo and draw a long loop through, yo and draw a loop through 2 loops on hook] 16 times, join with a slip stitch to 1-ch at beginning of round.

Round 4 Ch 1, [skip next st, 1 sc in next st] 8 times, join with a slip stitch to 1-ch at beginning of round.

Fasten off, leaving a long loose end.

To finish

Weave in the loose end of the base ring, but leave the finishing long loose end.

Sew the selected jewel (or button) to the center of the front of the motif.

Using the remaining long loose end, work an overcast stitch in each stitch all around the outer edge of the last round of the motif, pull to gather, and secure.

Cut a small circle from the scrap of leather or felt and sew a brooch pin to the center, using a matching sewing thread. Sew this piece to the back of the crochet motif.

Masterclass

Making a ball button

The technique I have used here to make these three-dimensional motif brooches is the same as you might use to make a crocheted ball button. By using this technique you can make a firm button simply using yarn and a hook, without the need for a plastic or metal foundation ring. You can vary the size and thickness of the motif or button depending on the weight of yarn used.

Make your ball button following the instructions for the small brooch on page 96. To begin, work the base ring and rounds 1 and 2. On round 3 work the single crochet stitches through the center of the button as shown in step 1 below. When working round 4, you will see how decreasing stitches draws the button into a ball shape (see step 2 below). Fasten off leaving a 12in-/30cm-long loose end.

Thread the long end onto a tapestry needle. Work an overcast stitch through each outside stitch, then pull the stitches together. Tie the beginning and end strands together, then sew an "X" across the button back for attaching to the garment.

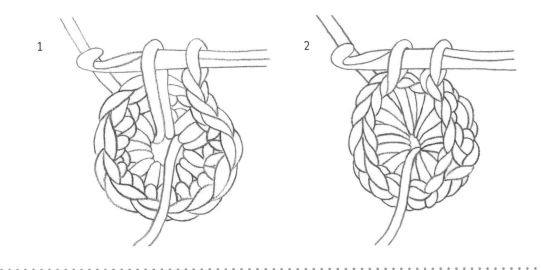

Round rug

The extreme yarn used to make this rug is an industrial waste product—the selvages from woven wool. Putting to use this by-product of the fabric trade, I have worked in the round on an oversized hook to match the yarn's scale. Crocheting knotted fabric strips creates a similarly unique textile.

Skill level

INTERMEDIATE

In this project you will learn
Using extreme yarn and a large hook
Working a large-scale flat motif in the round
How to make yarn from fabric strips, see
  masterclass on page 102

Stitches used
Single crochet

Size
Approximately 35½in/90cm in diameter

Materials
Thrum yarn consisting of a continuous 1in-/2.5cm-wide strip of patterned woven wool fabric, such as Ingrid Wagner Big Knit Yarn **6** SUPER BULKY in five colors:
  A 1 x 17½oz/500g ball (23yd/21m per ball) in first dark color
  B 1 x 17½oz/500g ball (23yd/21m per ball) in first neutral color
  C 1 x 17½oz/500g ball (23yd/21m per ball) in second dark color
  D 1 x 17½oz/500g ball (23yd/21m per ball) in second neutral color
  E 1 x 17½oz/500g ball (23yd/21m per ball) in third dark color
Size U (25mm) crochet hook

Gauge
3 sts and 3 rows to 4in/10cm measured over single crochet using a U (25mm) hook.

Abbreviations
See page 45.

Special pattern note
Mark the first chain at the beginning of every round with a colored thread.

To make rug
Base ring Using a U (25mm) hook and A, ch 4 and join with a slip stitch to first chain to form a ring.
Round 1 (RS) Using A, ch 1 (counts as first sc), 5 sc in ring, join with a slip stitch to first ch. *6 sts.*
Note: Do not turn at end of rounds but continue with RS of rug always facing.
Round 2 Using A, ch 1 (counts as first sc), 1 sc in same place as last slip stitch, *2 sc in next sc; rep from * to end of round, join with a slip stitch to first ch. *12 sts.*
Round 3 Using B, ch 1 (counts as first sc), 1 sc in same place as last slip stitch, 1 sc in next sc, *2 sc in next sc, 1 sc in next sc; rep from * to end of round, join with a slip stitch to first ch. *18 sts.*
Round 4 Using B, ch 1 (counts as first sc), 1 sc in same place as last slip stitch, 1 sc in each of next 2 sc, *2 sc in next sc, 1 sc in each of next 2 sc; rep from * to end of round, join with a slip stitch to first ch. *24 sts.*
Round 5 Using B, ch 1 (counts as first sc), 1 sc in same place as last slip stitch, 1 sc in each of next 3 sc, *2 sc in next sc, 1 sc in each of next 3 sc; rep from * to end of round, join with a slip stitch to first ch. *30 sts.*
Round 6 Using B, ch 1 (counts as first sc), 1 sc in same place as last slip stitch, 1 sc in each of next 4 sc, *2 sc in next sc, 1 sc in each of next 4 sc; rep from * to end of round, join with a slip stitch to first ch. *36 sts.*
Round 7 Using B, ch 1 (counts as first sc), 1 sc in same place as last slip stitch, 1 sc in each of next 5 sc, *2 sc in next sc, 1 sc in each of next 5 sc; rep from * to end of round, join with a slip stitch to first ch. *42 sts.*
Round 8 Using C, ch 1 (counts as first sc), 1 sc in

same place as last slip stitch, 1 sc in each of next 6 sc, *2 sc in next sc, 1 sc in each of next 6 sc; rep from * to end of round, join with a slip stitch to first ch. *48 sts.*

Round 9 Using D, ch 1 (counts as first sc), 1 sc in same place as last slip stitch, 1 sc in each of next 7 sc, *2 sc in next sc, 1 sc in each of next 7 sc; rep from * to end of round, join with a slip stitch to first ch. *54 sts.*

Round 10 Using D, ch 1 (counts as first sc), 1 sc in same place as last slip stitch, 1 sc in each of next 8 sc, *2 sc in next sc, 1 sc in each of next 8 sc; rep from * to end of round, join with a slip stitch to first ch. *60 sts.*

Round 11 Using D, ch 1 (counts as first sc), 1 sc in

same place as last slip stitch, 1 sc in each of next 9 sc, *2 sc in next sc, 1 sc in each of next 9 sc; rep from * to end of round, join with a slip stitch to first ch. *66 sts.*

Round 12 Using E, ch 1 (counts as first sc), 1 sc in same place as last slip stitch, 1 sc in each of next 10 sc, *2 sc in next sc, 1 sc in each of next 10 sc; rep from * to end of round, join with a slip stitch to first ch. *72 sts.*

Round 13 Using E, ch 1 (counts as first sc), 1 sc in same place as last slip stitch, 1 sc in each of next 11 sc, *2 sc in next sc, 1 sc in each of next 11 sc; rep from * to end of round, join with a slip stitch to first ch. *78 sts.*

Fasten off.

Masterclass

Making yarn from fabric strips

Making your own fabric yarn is as simple as cutting and knotting together fabric strips.

1 Lay each piece of fabric on a flat surface and using sharp scissors begin to cut into strips approximately 1in/2.5cm wide.

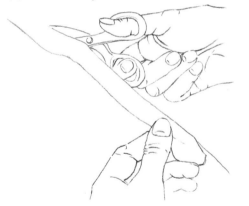

2 When you reach the end of the strip, stop approximately $\frac{1}{2}$in/1cm from the edge. Start cutting the next strip 1in/2.5cm along. This creates a continuous strip of fabric.

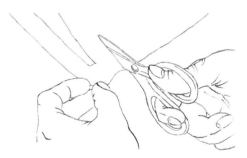

3 Cut each piece of fabric in this way to make long strips of each color or pattern. Start to wind the first fabric strip into a ball. Join the next strip with a double knot and continue to wind into a ball. The knots will form part of the crocheted textile.

4 Work a foundation chain in the usual way, however you may need to pay closer attention to how tightly you crochet, depending on the fabric, which may or may not be a little stretchy. Do not work the chains too tightly.

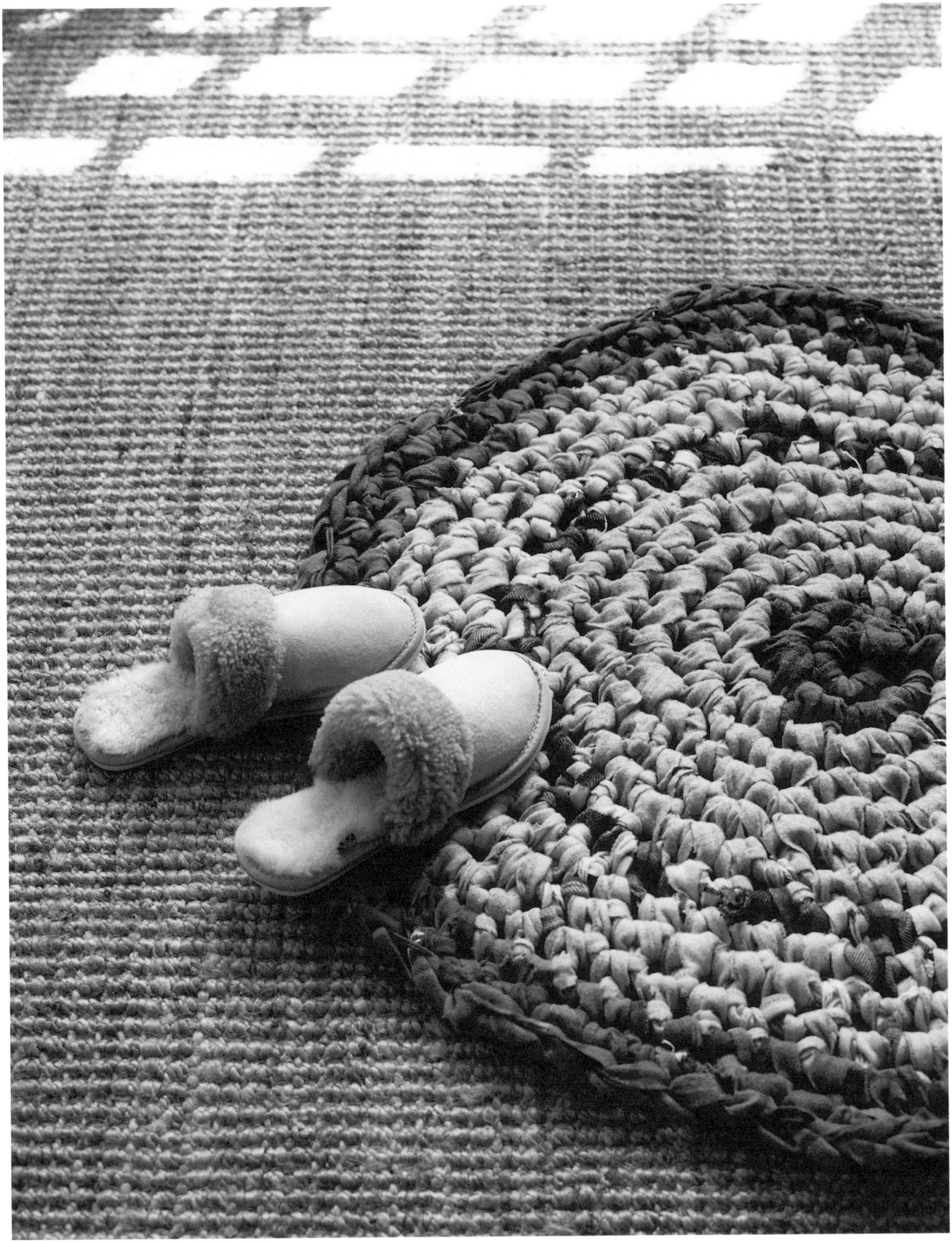

Rag pet bed

With two cats and a dog sharing my home, I know you can never have too many pet beds to avoid territorial turf conflict. To maintain household harmony, I periodically make this simple project. Worked in knotted strips of complimentary fabrics using single and double crochet, this is an inexpensive bed for four-legged friends.

Skill level

INTERMEDIATE

In this project you will learn
Working an external decrease
How to create a three-dimensional shape in the round

Stitches used
Single crochet; Double crochet

Size
Approximately 20in/50cm in diameter x 8³/₄in/22cm tall

Materials
Four different fabrics for making your own yarn
(6) SUPER BULKY :
  2¹/₄yd/2m natural linen fabric
  2¹/₄yd/2m black and white cotton gingham
  1¹/₄yd/1m calico
  2¹/₄yd/2m black and white striped heavy cotton fabric
Sizes M-13 (9mm) and N-15 (10mm) crochet hooks
Optional—round pillow form, 20in/50cm in diameter

Gauge
Approximately 7 sts and 8 rows to 4in/10cm measured over single crochet using an N-15 (10mm) hook and ⁵/₈in-/1.5cm-wide fabric strips.

Abbreviations
See page 45.

Special yarn strip notes
If necessary, wash the fabrics you are cutting into yarn strips first to take the "dressing" out to aid crocheting. Alternatively, you may prefer the more solid characteristic of the dressed material. Before starting to work, cut some long ⁵/₈in-/1.5cm-wide strips on the straight grain from each of the fabrics. Cut more strips as you need them. See masterclass on page 102 for tips on cutting "yarn" strips.

To make pet bed
Start with any strip of fabric and use different fabrics at random, changing at any stage by just knotting the two strips together.
Bed base
Base ring Using an N-15 (10mm) hook and a ⁵/₈in-/1.5cm- wide strip of fabric, ch 6 and join with a slip stitch to first chain to form a ring.
Round 1 (RS) Ch 3 (these first 3-ch count as first dc of each round), 11 dc in ring, join with a slip stitch to top of 3-ch at beginning of round. *12 sts.*
Note: Do not turn at end of rounds but continue with RS of work always facing.
Round 2 Ch 3, 1 dc in same place as last slip stitch, *2 dc in next dc; rep from * to end of round, join with a slip stitch to top of 3-ch at beginning of round. *24 sts.*
Round 3 Ch 3, 1 dc in same place as last slip stitch, 1 dc in next dc, *2 dc in next dc, 1 dc in next dc; rep from * to end, join with a slip stitch to top of 3-ch. *36 sts.*
Round 4 Ch 3, 1 dc in same place as last slip stitch, 1 dc in each of next 2 dc, *2 dc in next dc, 1 dc in each of next 2 dc; rep from * to end, join with a slip stitch to top of 3-ch. *48 sts.*
Round 5 Ch 3, 1 dc in same place as last slip stitch, 1 dc in each of next 3 dc, *2 dc in next dc, 1 dc in each of next 3 dc; rep from * to end, join with a slip stitch to top of 3-ch. *60 sts.*
Round 6 Ch 3, 1 dc in same place as last slip stitch, 1 dc in each of next 4 dc, *2 dc in next dc, 1 dc in each of next 4 dc; rep from * to end, join

with a slip stitch to top of 3-ch. *72 sts.*

Round 7 Ch 3, 1 dc in same place as last slip stitch, 1 dc in each of next 5 dc, *2 dc in next dc, 1 dc in each of next 5 dc; rep from * to end, join with a slip stitch to top of 3-ch. *84 sts.*

Round 8 Ch 3, 1 dc in same place as last slip stitch, 1 dc in each of next 6 dc, *2 dc in next dc, 1 dc in each of next 6 dc; rep from * to end, join with a slip stitch to top of 3-ch. *96 sts.*

Round 9 Ch 3, 1 dc in same place as last slip stitch, 1 dc in each of next 7 dc, *2 dc in next dc, 1 dc into each of next 7 dc; rep from * to end, join with a slip stitch to top of 3-ch. *108 sts.*
This completes the round base of the pet bed.

Begin sides of bed
The sides of the pet bed are worked in single crochet as follows:

Round 10 Ch 1, 1 sc in same place as last slip stitch, 1 sc in each dc to end of round, join with a slip stitch to first sc.

Round 11 Ch 1, 1 sc in same place as last slip stitch, 1 sc in each sc to end of round, join with a slip stitch to first sc.
Repeat last round until side measures 5in/12.5cm.

Shape sides
The rest of the pet bed is worked in rows to shape the front.
Place a marker on the 1-ch at the beg of sc section of every row as it helps you to see the start and finish of each row.

Next row (WS) Turn the work so the WS is facing, ch 1, 1 slip stitch in each of first 16 sc, ch 1 (place marker), 1 sc in each sc to end, turn. *92 sc.*

Next row Ch 1, 1 slip stitch in each of first 2 sc, ch 1 (place marker), 1 sc in each sc to end, turn.
Repeat the last row 5 times more.
Fasten off.

To finish

Tidy up any loose strip ends by weaving them into the work, although I like to leave the knots as a detail.

Edging
Using an M-13 (9mm) hook, join a strip with a slip stitch to a stitch at center of back, ch 1, 1 sc in same place as slip stitch, then work 1 sc in each st all around edge, join with a slip stitch to first sc.
Fasten off.

To make optional cushion cover

This cover is made from leftover fabric.
Front
Draw a circle 21in/53cm in diameter on a piece of paper and cut out the circle. Cut one piece of fabric using this paper pattern piece.
Back pieces
To make the paper pattern for the two back pieces, fold the paper pattern for the front in half along the diameter. Unfold, draw a line 4in/10cm from fold and cut along this line. Cut two pieces of fabric using this pattern piece. Make a narrow double hem along both straight edges of the back pieces.
Sewing back pieces to front
Place one back piece on top of the front piece with right sides together and the outer edges aligned. Place second back piece on the front so that it overlaps the first piece at the center. Pin the back pieces to the front and stitch all around leaving a 1/2in/1.5cm seam allowance. Clip the curves, turn right side out, and press. Insert the pillow form.

Masterclass

Working an external decrease
This is a method for decreasing more than one stitch at an external edge, such as the sloped front edge of the pet bed.

To decrease at the beginning of the row, work a slip stitch into each of the stitches to be decreased, then work the appropriate turning chain and continue along the row. To decrease at the end of the row, simply leave the stitches to be decreased unworked, turn, then work the appropriate turning chain and continue along the row.

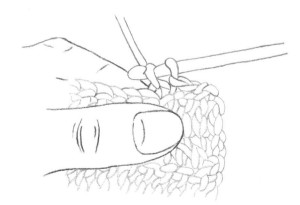

Two-color bolster

The intricate visual effect of this two-color "Catherine Wheel" stitch belies the simplicity of the pattern. Only one color is ever worked at a time, but the broken stripe design creates an interesting textile. The ends of this bolster are simply rounds worked into spaces and finished with a scallop edging.

Skill level

■■■□
EXPERIENCED

In this project you will learn
A two-color stitch; Working a scallop edging

Stitches used
Single crochet; Double crochet; Treble crochet; Double crochet shells; Double crochet clusters

Size
Approximately 17¾in/45cm long x 6¾in/17cm in diameter

Materials
Super-fine-weight mercerized cotton yarn, such as Yeoman Yarns Cotton Cannele 4-ply SUPER FINE in two colors:
 A 1 x 9oz/245g cone (930yd/850m per cone) in dark gray
 B 1 x 9oz/245g cone (930yd/850m per cone) in aqua blue
Size D-3 (3mm) crochet hook
Bolster 17¾in/45cm long x 6¾in/17cm in diameter
Two ¾in/22mm dark shell buttons

Gauge
28 sts and 13 rows to 4in/10cm measured over two-color stitch pattern using a D-3 (3mm) hook.

Abbreviations
1 cluster = [yo, insert hook in next stitch, yo and draw a loop through, yo and draw through first 2 loops on hook] over the number of stitches indicated, yo and draw a loop through all loops on hook to complete cluster.
See also page 45.

Special pattern note
To work a gauge swatch in the two-color stitch pattern, make a multiple of 10 chains, plus 7 chains extra, for the foundation chain—37 chains will be sufficient. Using a D-3 (3mm) hook, work rows 1–5 of the pattern, then repeat rows 2–5 until the swatch measures approximately 5in/13cm long. This will create a swatch big enough to test your gauge.

To make main part of bolster cover
The foundation chain and the first row of the two-color stitch pattern (called "Catherine Wheel" stitch) are worked in A, thereafter two rows each in B and A are repeated. When changing color, weave in the yarn ends.
Foundation chain Using a D-3 (3mm) hook and A, ch 127.
Row 1 (RS) Using A, 1 sc in 2nd ch from hook, 1 sc in next ch, *skip 3 ch, 7 dc in next ch (these 7 dc in same chain form a 7-dc shell), skip 3 ch, 1 sc in each of next 3 ch; rep from * to last 4 ch, skip 3 ch, 4 dc in last ch, turn.
Row 2 Using B, ch 1, 1 sc in each of first 2 dc, *ch 3, 1 cluster over next 7 sts (that is over next 2 dc, 3 sc, 2 dc), ch 3, 1 sc in each of next 3 dc (these 3 dc are the 3 center sts of the 7-dc shell); rep from * to last 4 sts (remaining 2 dc and 2 sc), finishing with ch 3, 1 cluster over these last 4 sts, turn.
Row 3 Using B, ch 3 (counts as first dc), 3 dc in top of first 4-dc cluster (under loop that closes the cluster), *skip 3-ch sp, 1 sc in each of next 3 sc, skip 3-ch sp, 7 dc in top of next cluster (under loop that closed the cluster); rep from * to last 3-ch sp, finishing with skip 3-ch sp, 1 sc in each of last 2 sc, turn.
Row 4 Using A, ch 3 (counts as first dc) skip first sc, 1 cluster over next 3 sts (that is over next 1 sc, 2 dc), *ch 3, 1 sc in each of next 3 dc (these 3 dc are the 3 center sts of the 7-dc shell), ch 3, 1 cluster over next 7 sts (that is over next 2 dc,

hanging at the back of the work to pick up for the next round.

Base ring Using a D-3 (3mm) hook and A, ch 4 and join with a slip stitch to first chain to form a ring.

Round 1 (RS) Using A, ch 3, 2 dc in ring (counts as first 3-dc group), work [ch 1, 3 dc] 3 times in ring, ch 1, join with a slip stitch to top of 3-ch at beginning of round. *4 3-dc groups.*

Note: Do not turn at end of rounds but continue with RS of work always facing.

Round 2 Using B, ch 3, 2 dc in last ch sp of last round (counts as first 3-dc group), 3 dc in next dc, [3 dc in next ch sp, 3 dc in center dc of next 3-dc group] 3 times, join with a slip stitch to top of 3-ch at beginning of round. *8 3-dc groups.*

Round 3 Using A, ch 3, 2 dc in sp between first and last 3-dc groups of previous round (counts as first 3-dc group), 3 dc in next dc, [3 dc in each of next 2 sps (*sps* and *sp* henceforth refer to the spaces between the 3-dc groups), 3 dc in center dc of next 3-dc group] 3 times, 3 dc in next sp, join with a slip stitch to top of 3-ch. *12 3-dc groups.*

Round 4 Using B, ch 3, 2 dc in sp between first and last 3-dc groups, 3 dc in each of next 2 sps, [3 dc in center dc of next 3-dc group, 3 dc in each of next 3 sps] 3 times, 3 dc in center dc of next 3-dc group, join with a slip stitch to top of 3-ch. *16 3-dc groups.*

Round 5 Using A, ch 3, 2 dc in sp between first and last 3-dc groups, 3 dc in next sp, [3 dc in center dc of next 3-dc group, 3 dc in each of next 4 sps] 3 times, 3 dc in center dc of next 3-dc group, 3 dc in each of next 2 sps, join with a slip stitch to top of 3-ch. *20 3-dc groups.*

Round 6 Using B, ch 3, 2 dc in sp between first and last 3-dc groups, 3 dc in each of next 3 sps, [3 dc in center dc of next 3-dc group, 3 dc in each

3 sc, 2 dc); rep from * to last dc, finishing with ch 3, 1 sc in last dc, 1 sc in top of 3-ch at end of row, turn.

Row 5 Using A, ch 1, 1 sc in each of first 2 sc, *skip 3-ch sp, 7 dc in top of next cluster, skip 3-ch sp, 1 sc in each of next 3 sc; rep from * to last 3-ch sp, finishing with skip 3-ch sp, 4 dc in top of 3-ch at end of row, turn.

Repeat rows 2–5 to form two-color stitch pattern and continue in pattern until work measures 21³/₄in/55cm from beginning, ending with a row 4. Fasten off.

To make bolster cover ends (make 2)

The bolster cover ends are also worked in two colors, alternating one round A and one round B. Do not cut off the yarn not in use but leave it

Stitch diagram Catherine Wheel Stitch

KEY

o = chain stitch

+ = single crochet

⊤ = double crochet

🌟 = cluster

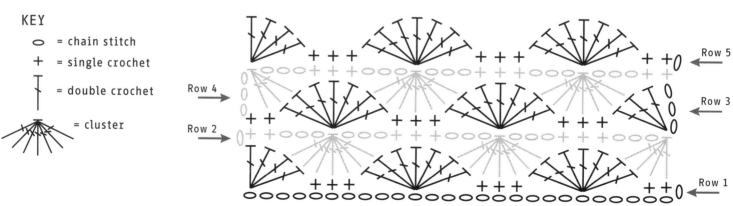

of next 5 sps] 3 times, 3 dc in center dc of next 3-dc group, 3 dc in next sp, join with a slip stitch to top of 3-ch. *24 3-dc groups.*

Round 7 Using A, ch 3, 2 dc in sp between first and last 3-dc groups, 3 dc in next sp, [3 dc in center dc of next 3-dc group, 3 dc in each of next 6 sps] 3 times, 3 dc in center dc of next 3-dc group, 3 dc in each of next 4 sps, join with a slip stitch to top of 3-ch. *28 3-dc groups.*

Round 8 Using B, ch 3, 2 dc in sp between first and last 3-dc groups, 3 dc in each of next 6 sps, [3 dc in center dc of next 3-dc group, 3 dc in each of next 7 sps] 3 times, 3 dc in center dc of next 3-dc group, join with a slip stitch to top of 3-ch. *32 3-dc groups.*

Round 9 Using A, ch 3, 2 dc in sp between first and last 3-dc groups, 3 dc in each of next 3 sps, [3 dc in center dc of next 3-dc group, 3 dc in each of next 8 sps] 3 times, 3 dc in center dc of next 3-dc group, 3 dc in each of next 4 sps, join with a slip stitch to top of 3-ch. *36 3-dc groups.*

Round 10 Using B, ch 3, 2 dc in sp between first and last 3-dc groups, 3 dc in each of next 5 sps, [3 dc in center dc of next 3-dc group, 3 dc in each of next 9 sps] 3 times, 3 dc in center dc of next 3-dc group, 3 dc in each of next 3 sps, join with a slip stitch to top of 3-ch. *40 3-dc groups.* Fasten off.

Edging
With RS of work facing and using a D-3 (3mm) hook and B, join yarn with a slip stitch to any stitch on the edge of the end piece and work as follows:
Skip next 2 sts, work [2 dc, ch 1, 1 tr, ch 1, 2 dc] all in next st, *skip next 2 sts, 1 slip stitch in next st, skip next 2 sts, work [2 dc, ch 1, 1 tr, ch 1, 2 dc] all in next st; rep from * to end, join with a slip stitch to first slip stitch. Fasten off.
Make second end piece in exactly the same way.

To finish
Weave in any loose ends.
Lay work out flat and gently steam on wrong side. Sew together the first and last rows of main piece. Sew on one end all around, keeping edging free and on the outside of the bolster cover. Insert the feather bolster and sew on the second end as before.
Sew one button to center of each end.

Masterclass

Working a scallop edging
Adding a crochet border lends a final decorative touch; it can be worked not only on a piece of crochet but also knitting and even woven fabric. To work this shell edging you need a foundation row to work into. If your piece does not already have a suitable foundation row, make a row or round of single crochet. When crocheting this border, take care to ensure that the right side of the shell edging ends up facing the correct way.

1 Ensure that the foundation row is a multiple of 6 stitches. Join the yarn to the edge with a slip stitch, skip 2 stitches, then *work 2 double crochet, chain 1, 1 treble, chain 1, 2 double crochet into the next stitch.

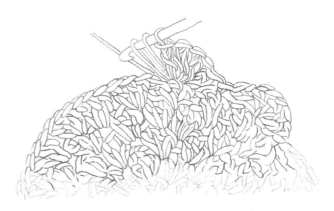

2 Skip 2 stitches, 1 slip stitch in next stitch, skip 2 stitches. Continue by repeating from * to end of the round or row. When the edging is complete, join with a slip stitch to the first slip stitch.

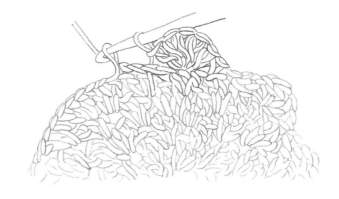

Traditional square motif throw

At the heart of this throw are two traditional motifs. Also known as a "granny square," this motif is a basic every new crocheter should master. Sewn together, these motifs form the rectangular center around which the remaining rounds are worked resulting in a perfect throw for a bed or sofa.

Skill level

■■■□
INTERMEDIATE

In this project you will learn
Making a simple square motif

Stitches used
Double crochet

Size
Approximately 44in/111.5cm wide x 47³/₄in/121cm long

Materials
Fine-weight cotton yarn, such as Rowan Cotton Glacé (2) FINE in 11 colors:

A 3 x 1³/₄oz/50g balls (125yd/115m per ball) in olive
B 2 x 1³/₄oz/50g balls (125yd/115m per ball) in wine red
C 3 x 1³/₄oz/50g balls (125yd/115m per ball) in brown
D 1 x 1³/₄oz/50g balls (125yd/115m per ball) in dusty lilac
E 3 x 1³/₄oz/50g balls (125yd/115m per ball) in light brown
F 1 x 1³/₄oz/50g balls (125yd/115m per ball) in grape
G 2 x 1³/₄oz/50g balls (125yd/115m per ball) in pale pink
H 2 x 1³/₄oz/50g balls (125yd/115m per ball) in medium pink
J 3 x 1³/₄oz/50g balls (125yd/115m per ball) in dark mauve
K 2 x 1³/₄oz/50g balls (125yd/115m per ball) in dark gray
L 2 x 1³/₄oz/50g balls (125yd/115m per ball) in blue-green

Sizes C-2 (2.5mm) and D-3 (3mm) crochet hooks

Gauge
One basic granny square measures 3³/₄in/9.5cm x 3³/₄in/9.5cm using a D-3 (3mm) hook.
5 3-dc groups and 9¹/₂ rows to 4in/10cm measured over main pattern using a D-3 (3mm) hook.

Abbreviations
See page 45.

Stitch diagram
See page 57 for the symbol diagram for the square motif.

To make throw
The center of the throw is worked first and is made up of two basic square motifs stitched together side by side, then the main throw is worked around this rectangular center.

Basic square motifs (make 2)
Base ring Using a D-3 (3mm) hook and A, ch 6 and join with a slip stitch to first chain to form a ring.
Round 1 (RS) Using A, ch 3 (counts as first dc), 2 dc in ring, [ch 3, 3 dc in ring] 3 times, ch 3, join with a slip stitch to top of 3-ch at beginning of round. Fasten off.
Round 2 Using B, join yarn with a slip stitch to any 3-ch sp, ch 3 (counts as first dc), [2 dc, ch 3, 3 dc] in same 3-ch sp, *ch 1, [3 dc, ch 3, 3 dc] in next 3-ch sp; rep from * twice more, ch 1, join with a slip stitch to top of 3-ch at beginning of round. Fasten off.
Round 3 Using C, join yarn with a slip stitch to any 3-ch sp, ch 3 (counts as first dc), [2 dc, ch 3, 3 dc] in same 3-ch sp, *ch 1, 3 dc in next 1-ch sp, ch 1, [3 dc, ch 3, 3 dc] in next 3-ch sp; rep from * twice more, ch 1, 3 dc in next 1-ch sp, ch 1, join

with a slip stitch to top of 3-ch at beginning of round. Fasten off.

Round 4 Using D, join on yarn with a slip stitch to any 3-ch sp, ch 3 (counts as first dc), [2 dc, ch 3, 3 dc] in same 3-ch sp, *[ch 1, 3 dc in next 1-ch sp] twice, ch 1, [3 dc, ch 3, 3 dc] in next 3-ch sp; rep from * twice more, [ch 1, 3 dc in next 1-ch sp] twice, ch 1, join with a slip stitch to top of 3-ch at beginning of round. Fasten off.

Work second basic square motif in same way, but use E for base ring and round 1, F for round 2, A for round 3, and G for round 4.

Main section

To form the rectangular throw center, sew the two basic square motifs together along one side using neat overcast stitches. Work the remainder of the throw around this rectangle as follows:

Round 1 (RS) With RS of work facing and using F, join on yarn with a slip stitch to a 3-ch sp at the beg of a long edge, then work ch 3 (counts as first dc), [2 dc, ch 3, 3 dc] in same 3-ch sp, [ch 1, 3 dc in next 1-ch sp] 8 times, ch 1, [3 dc, ch 3, 3 dc] in next 3-ch sp, [ch 1, 3 dc in next 1-ch sp] 3 times, ch 1, [3 dc, ch 3, 3 dc] into next 3-ch sp, [ch 1, 3 dc in next 1-ch sp] 8 times, ch 1, [3 dc, ch 3, 3 dc] in next 3-ch sp, [ch 1, 3 dc in next 1-ch sp] 3 times, ch 1, join with a slip stitch to top of 3-ch at beginning of round. Fasten off.

Round 2 Using H, join on yarn with a slip stitch to any 3-ch sp, ch 3 (counts as first dc), [2 dc, ch 3, 3 dc] in same 3-ch sp, *[ch 1, 3 dc] in each 1-ch sp until you reach the next 3-ch corner sp, ch 1,

[3 dc, ch 3, 3 dc] in this 3-ch sp; rep from * twice more, [ch 1, 3 dc] in each 1-ch sp to the end of the round, ch 1, join with a slip stitch to top of 3-ch at beginning of round. Fasten off.

Repeat round 2 for 46 rounds more, changing color each round and using the following colors:
Round 3 E; **round 4** J; **round 5** A; **round 6** E; **round 7** G; **round 8** K; **round 9** C; **round 10** B; **round 11** D; **round 12** F; **round 13** A; **round 14** L; **round 15** G; **round 16** E; **round 17** H; **round 18** J; **round 19** C; **round 20** K; **round 21** L; **round 22** H; **round 23** A; **round 24** F; **round 25** D; **round 26** A; **round 27** B; **round 28** E; **round 29** G; **round 30** J; **round 31** F; **round 32** L; **round 33** H; **round 34** C; **round 35** K; **round 36** B; **round 37** C; **round 38** G; **round 39** J; **round 40** A; **round 41** K; **round 42** E; **round 43** H; **round 44** J; **round 45** L; **round 46** A; **round 47** C; **round 48** J. Fasten off.

Throw now measures approximately 43$\frac{1}{2}$in/110.5cm x 47$\frac{1}{4}$in/120cm.

To finish

Weave in any loose ends.

Edging

Using a C-2 hook and E, join yarn with a slip stitch to any 3-ch sp on outside edge of throw, ch 3, [2 dc, ch 3, 3 dc] in same 3-ch sp, then work 1 dc in each dc, 1 dc in each 1-ch sp and [3 dc, ch 3, 3 dc] in each corner sp to end, join with a slip stitch to top of 3-ch at beginning of round. Fasten off.

Lay work out flat and gently steam on wrong side.

Masterclass

Choosing yarns and colors for a project

The success of a crochet project more often than not hinges on the quality of the yarn selected as well as the color palette. Traditional square motifs—or "granny squares"—such as the ones at the center of this throw are most often worked in wool, which gives a soft feel and a fluid textile. However, I have chosen a natural cotton yarn for this project as it gives good stitch clarity, has an attractive sheen, and takes dye well so offers good clean colors. When considering a yarn, work up a large swatch and ask yourself a series of questions: Is it too heavy or too light? Is it soft to the touch? Do I like the overall effect? Whether designing garments, accessories, or homewares, I lean toward an understated color palette of muted tones. Preferring to use the characteristic colors of natural yarns as a base, I usually introduce stronger colors as highlights within the overall scheme. For this Traditional Motif Throw, a base of browns, grays, and olive green provide a quiet backdrop for the punchier reds, pinks, and plum. A zesty lime is one of my favorite accent colors to juxtapose soft ecru, fawn, brown, and gray. Or for a classic colorway, team mid-blue with earthy browns. An alternative colorway comprising a range of tonal grays would be an equally chic choice for this project.

Motif tablemats

Here's a simple and practical way to learn how to crochet three different round motifs. Each is made in cotton, worked in subtle, complementary neutral tones, to create a stylish, crafty, and contemporary addition to the "top of table." A wonderfully inexpensive house gift!

Skill level

INTERMEDIATE

In this project you will learn
Working intricate motifs

Stitches used
Single crochet; Half double crochet;
Double crochet; Treble crochet; Puff stitch;
Double crochet clusters

Size
Each tablemat measures approximately 8in/20cm in diameter

Materials
Double-knitting-weight cotton yarn, such as
Rowan Handknit Cotton ③ LIGHT in desired color:
  1 x 1³/₄oz/50g ball (93yd/85m per ball) for each
  tablemat motif in one of these colors—light
  sage green, bluey lilac, ecru, purple, or taupe
Size H-8 (5mm) crochet hook

Gauge
Each finished motif measures approximately 8in/20cm in diameter using an H-8 hook and yarn double.

Abbreviations
1 puff stitch = [yo, insert hook in ring and draw a long loop through] twice, yo and draw a loop through all 5 loops on hook.
1 cluster = [yo and insert hook in next dc, yo and draw a loop through, yo and draw through first 2 loops on hook] 5 times, yo and draw a loop through all 6 loops on hook.

dc4tog = [yo and insert hook in next dc, yo and draw a loop through, yo and draw through first 2 loops on hook] 4 times, yo and draw a loop through all 5 loops on hook.
See also page 45.

Special yarn note
Use two strands of yarn held together throughout.

To make wagon wheel tablemat
This tablemat is shown worked in three different colors—light sage green, taupe, and bluey lilac.
Base ring Using an H-8 (5mm) hook and yarn double, ch 4 and join with a slip stitch to first chain to form a ring.
Round 1 (RS) Ch 3 and 1 hdc in ring (counts as first puff st), ch 1, [1 puff stitch, ch 1] 7 times in ring, join with a slip stitch to top of 3-ch at beginning of round. *8 petals.*
Round 2 1 slip stitch in next hdc, 1 slip stitch in next ch sp, ch 3, 1 dc in same ch sp as last slip stitch, ch 2, [2 dc, ch 2] in each of next 7 ch sps, join with a slip stitch to top of 3-ch at beginning of round.
Round 3 1 slip stitch in next dc, 1 slip stitch in next ch sp, ch 3, [1 dc, ch 1, 2 dc] in same ch sp as last slip stitch, ch 1, [2 dc, ch 1] twice in each of next 7 ch sps, join with a slip stitch to top of 3-ch at beginning of round.
Round 4 1 slip stitch in next dc, 1 slip stitch in next ch sp, ch 3, 2 dc in same ch sp as last slip stitch, ch 1, [3 dc, ch 1] in each of next 15 ch sps, join with a slip stitch to top of 3-ch at beginning of round.
Round 5 1 slip stitch in each of next 2 dc, 1 slip stitch in next ch sp, ch 3, 3 dc in same ch sp as last slip stitch, ch 1, [4 dc, ch 1] in each of next

15 ch sps, join with a slip stitch to top of 3-ch at beginning of round.
Round 6 1 slip stitch in each of next 3 dc, 1 slip stitch in next ch sp, ch 3, 3 dc in same ch sp as last slip stitch, ch 2, [4 dc, ch 2] in each of next 15 ch sps, join with a slip stitch to top of 3-ch at beginning of round.
Fasten off.

To make begonia wheel tablemat

This tablemat is shown worked two different colors—ecru and bluey lilac.
Base ring Using an H-8 (5mm) hook and yarn double, ch 6 and join with a slip stitch to first chain to form a ring.
Round 1 (RS) Ch 3 (counts as first dc), 13 dc in ring, join with a slip stitch to top of 3-ch at beginning of round.
Round 2 Ch 3 (counts as first dc), 2 dc in same place as last slip stitch, *ch 1, skip 1 dc, 3 dc in next dc; rep from * 5 times more, ch 1, join with a slip stitch to top of 3-ch at beginning of round.
Round 3 1 slip stitch in next dc, ch 3 (counts as first dc), 1 dc in same dc as slip stitch, *ch 1, 2 dc in next 1-ch sp, ch 1, skip 1 dc, 2 dc in next dc (center dc of 3-dc group); rep from * 5 times more, ch 1, 2 dc in next 1-ch sp, ch 1, join with a slip stitch to top of 3-ch at beginning of round.
Round 4 [Ch 4, 1 sc in next 1-ch sp] 13 times, ch 2, 1 dc in base of first 4-ch.
Round 5 [Ch 4, 1 sc in center of next 4-ch sp] 13

times, ch 2, 1 dc in dc at end of previous round.
Round 6 Ch 3 (counts as first dc), 3 dc in sp formed by dc at end of previous round, 4 dc in each of next 13 4-ch sps, join with a slip stitch to top of 3-ch at beginning of round.
Round 7 Ch 3, 1 dc in same place as last slip stitch, 1 dc in each of next 3 dc, *2 dc in next dc, 1 dc in each of next 3 dc; rep from * 12 times more, join with a slip stitch to top of 3-ch at beginning of round.
Fasten off.

To make ice crystal tablemat

This tablemat is shown worked in three different colors—ecru, light sage green, and purple.
Base ring Using an H-8 (5mm) hook and yarn double, ch 6 and join with a slip stitch to first chain to form a ring.
Round 1 (RS) Ch 1 (does NOT count as a stitch), 12 sc in ring, join with a slip stitch to first sc. *12 sc.*
Round 2 Ch 1 (does NOT count as a stitch), 1 sc in same place as last slip stitch, [ch 7, skip 1 sc, 1 sc in next sc] 5 times, ch 3, 1 tr in top of first sc.
Round 3 Ch 3, (counts as first dc), 4 dc in sp formed by tr at end of previous round, [ch 3, 5 dc in next 7-ch sp] 5 times, ch 3, join with a slip stitch to top of 3-ch at beginning of round.
Round 4 Ch 3 (counts as first dc), 1 dc in each of next 4 dc, *ch 3, 1 sc in next 3-ch sp, ch 3,** 1 dc in each of next 5 dc; rep from * 4 more times and from * to ** again, join with a slip stitch to top of 3-ch at beginning of round.
Round 5 Ch 3 and dc4tog over next 4 dc (counts as first cluster), *[ch 5, 1 sc in next 3-ch sp] twice, ch 5,** 1 cluster over next 5 dc; rep from * 4 more times and from * to ** again, join with a slip stitch top of first cluster.
Round 6 Ch 3, 4 dc in first 5-ch sp, [ch 2, 1 sc in next 5-ch sp, ch 2, 5 dc in next 5-ch sp, ch 2, 5 dc in next 5-ch sp] 5 times, ch 2, 1 sc in next 5-ch sp, ch 2, 5 dc in next 5-ch sp, ch 2, join with a slip stitch to top of 3-ch at beginning of round.
Fasten off.

To finish all motifs

Weave in any loose ends.
Lay work out flat and gently steam on wrong side.

Stitch diagram
Wagon Wheel

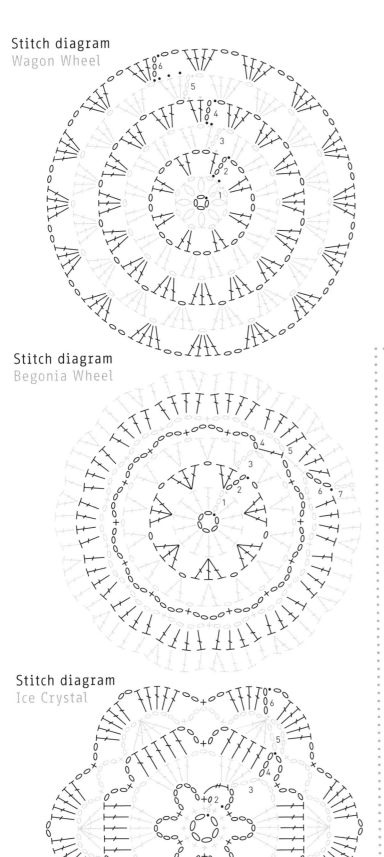

Stitch diagram
Begonia Wheel

Stitch diagram
Ice Crystal

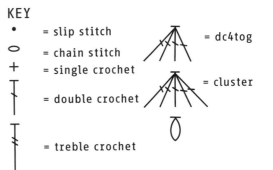

KEY

- • = slip stitch
- ○ = chain stitch
- + = single crochet
- ┼ = double crochet
- ╪ = treble crochet
- = dc4tog
- = cluster

Masterclass

Tips for working motifs

If you have never attempted making a motif, read the explanation on pages 38–39 about working in rounds. The Wagon Wheel motif is the easiest of the tablemats, so start with this one. It is also a very versatile motif, because you can stop after three rounds for a coaster or work all six rounds for the tablemat.

If you find it difficult to fit all the stitches of the first round into the base ring of the motif, which can happen with thick yarn, undo your work and start again. This time make the chains of the ring loosely or add one or two chains to make it bigger, and leave a long loose end at the beginning. Lay the yarn tail at the back of the motif, level with the chain ring, and work all the stitches of the first round over it—so it is captured inside the base of the stitches. Later you can pull the end to close up the hole at the center of the ring if you want to. It also means there is less weaving in later.

At the beginning of each round place a stitch marker on the first stitch, a safety pin or a colored thread will do. If you lose track of which round you are on, simply count the markers. Follow the symbol diagram as you work the rows; it is sometimes easier to understand than the written instructions.

Daisy-chain necklace

This impossibly pretty necklace is created from a long length of chain worked in fine linen yarn, which is embellished with individual leaf and flower motifs. I have added natural shell buttons at irregular intervals to introduce a contrasting texture but in a natural, tonal hue.

Skill level

EASY

In this project you will learn
Practicing even chain stitches
Making small flower and leaf motifs
Adding buttons and beads

Stitches used
Chain stitches; Single crochet; Half double crochet; Double crochet; Treble crochet

Size
Approximately 124in/315cm long—but this is easily adjustable to suit desired length

Materials
No. 10 linen crochet thread, such as Anchor Artiste Linen Crochet Thread No. 10 (2) FINE in one color:
    1 x 1³/₄oz/50g ball (289yd/265m per ball) in natural
Size B-1 (2mm) crochet hook
16 round two-hole natural shell buttons (eleven 8mm–11mm; five 14–18mm)

Gauge
There is no need to work to a specific gauge for this project.

Abbreviations
See page 45.

Special pattern notes
When working the flowers and leaves, leave a long end to use for attaching the motif to the chain. The number of motifs and buttons specified are just a suggestion; alter the numbers as desired.

To make necklace
Using a B-1 (2mm) hook, work a chain that measures approximately 124in/135cm. Fasten off. The chain should be long enough to wrap several times around your neck without the need for a clasp.

Five-petal flower (make 13)
Base ring Using a B-1 (2mm) hook, ch 4 and join with a slip stitch to first chain to form a ring.
Round 1 Ch 1, *1 sc in ring, ch 3, [yo and insert hook in ring, yo and draw a loop through, yo and draw through first 2 loops on hook] twice, yo and draw through all 3 loops on hook (called dc2tog), ch 3; rep from * 4 times more, join with a slip stitch to top of first sc. *5 petals made.*
Fasten off.

Shell-cluster flower (make 2)
Base ring Using a B-1 (2mm) hook, ch 4 and join with a slip stitch to first chain to form a ring.
Round 1 *Ch 3, 2 dc in ring, ch 3, 1 slip stitch in last dc worked (one picot made), 1 dc in ring, ch 3, 1 slip stitch in ring, ch 3, 3 dc in ring, ch 3, 1 slip stitch in ring; rep from * once more. *4 petals made.*
Fasten off.

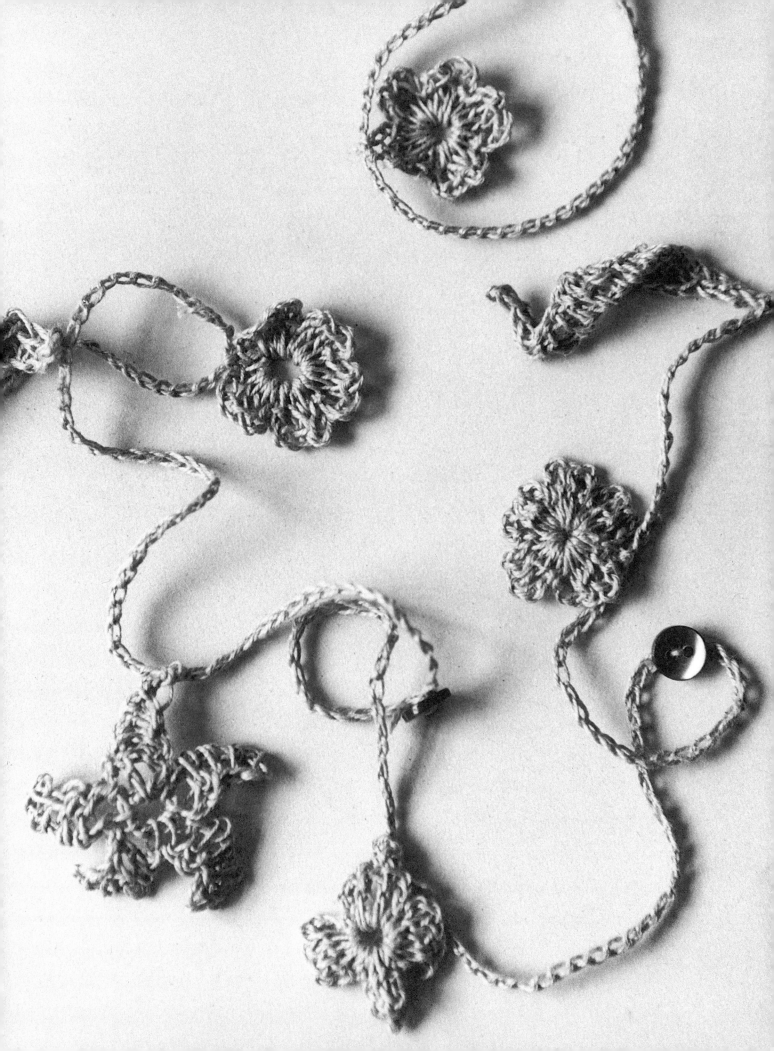

- = slip stitch
○ = chain stitch
+ = single crochet
⊤ = half double crochet
⊤ = double crochet
⋏ = dc2tog
⊥ = treble crochet

Stitch diagram Small Leaf

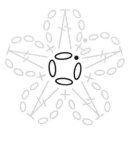

Row 1

Pointed flower (make 2)

Base ring Using a B-1 (2mm) hook, ch 4 and join with a slip stitch to first chain to form a ring.
Round 1 Ch 1, 1 sc in ring, *ch 5, 1 sc in 2nd ch from hook, 1 hdc in next ch, 1 dc in each of next 2 ch, 1 sc in ring; rep from * 3 times more, ch 5, 1 sc in 2nd ch from hook, 1 hdc in next ch, 1 dc in each of next 2 ch, join with a slip stitch to top of first sc.
Fasten off.

Small leaf (make 6)

Foundation chain Using a B-1 (2mm) hook, ch 13.
Row 1 Work 1 slip stitch in 2nd ch from hook, 1 sc in next ch, 1 hdc in next ch, 1 dc in each of next 2 ch, 1 tr in each of next 3 ch, 1 dc in next ch, 1 hdc into next ch, 1 sc in next ch, 1 slip stitch in last ch.
Fasten off.

To finish

Sew the two ends of the chain together. Weave in any loose ends, leaving the long finishing ends on the motifs.
Using the long ends, sew the motifs randomly to the length of chain. Using a matching sewing threads, sew the small natural shell buttons to the chain, intermingling them between the crochet motifs.

Stitch diagram
Five-petal Flower

Stitch diagram
Shell-cluster Flower

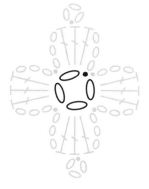

Stitch diagram Pointed Flower

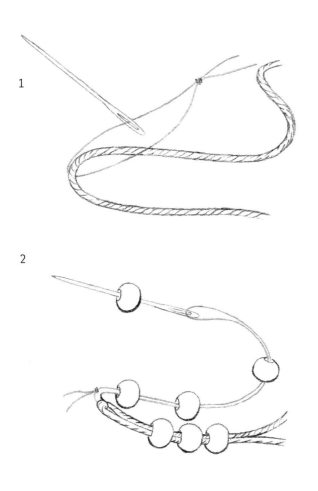

1

2

3

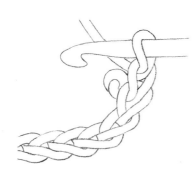

4

Crocheting beads and buttons into a chain
If you are crocheting your beads or buttons into the work, rather than sewing them on afterward, then it is essential that the beads or buttons are threaded onto the yarn before you begin to crochet.

1 Thread a fine sewing needle with sewing thread and make a small knot to join the ends and form a loop. Move the knot so that it is not in line horizontally with the sewing needle.

2 Place the end of the yarn through the loop created by the sewing thread, then pass the beads over the eye of the needle and push down onto the sewing thread and then onto the yarn. The first few beads may be a bit tricky, but so long as the bead holes are large enough, threading will become easier.

3 Make chains up to the stage where a bead or button is needed. Then slide the bead or button along the yarn so it sits next to the hook.

4 Work the next chain by wrapping the yarn over the hook beyond the bead or button and drawing it through the loop on the hook.

Patchwork motif blanket

This patchwork blanket is made up of the same square motif—210 motifs, in fact—randomly placed and sewn together. Working the separate rounds in one, two, three, or four colors has an intriguing optical effect, breaking up the motif and accentuating its rounder or squarer characteristics.

Skill level

INTERMEDIATE

In this project you will learn
Arranging colored motifs for a patchwork effect, see masterclass on page 126

Stitches used
Single crochet
Double crochet

Size
Approximately 50¹/₂in/128cm wide x 54in/137cm long

Materials
Super-fine-weight cashmere-and-wool-mix yarn, such as Rowan Cashsoft 4-Ply **(1)** SUPER FINE in 7 colors:

A 4 x 1³/₄oz/50g balls (197yd/180m per ball) in mauve
B 4 x 1³/₄oz/50g balls (197yd/180m per ball) in light brown
C 3 x 1³/₄oz/50g balls (197yd/180m per ball) in gray
D 5 x 1³/₄oz/50g balls (197yd/180m per ball) in pale putty
E 5 x 1³/₄oz/50g balls (197yd/180m per ball) in turquoise
F 3 x 1³/₄oz/50g balls (197yd/180m per ball) in dark brown
G 2 x 1³/₄oz/50g balls (197yd/180m per ball) in black
Sizes C-2 (2.5mm) and D-3 (3mm) crochet hooks

Gauge
Each square measures approximately 3¹/₂in/9cm x 3¹/₂in/9cm using a D-3 (3mm) hook.

Abbreviations
See page 45.

To make each square motif
See the blanket instructions for the colors.
Base ring Using a D-3 (3mm) hook and color required for round 1, ch 8 and join with a slip stitch to first chain to form a ring.
Round 1 (RS) Ch 3 (counts as first dc), 15 dc in ring, join with a slip stitch to top of 3-ch at beginning of round.
Round 2 Ch 5 (counts as first dc and 2-ch sp), [1 dc in next dc, ch 2] 15 times, join with a slip stitch to 3rd of 5-ch at beginning of round. *16 spokes.*
Round 3 Ch 3 (counts as first dc), 2 dc in first 2-ch sp, ch 1, [3 dc in next 2-ch sp, ch 1] 15 times, join with a slip stitch to top of 3-ch.
Round 4 1 slip stitch st in each of next 2 dc and next 1-ch sp, ch 1, 1 sc in same 1-ch sp as slip stitch, *[ch 3, 1 sc in next 1-ch sp] 3 times, ch 6, 1 sc in next 1-ch sp; rep from * 3 times more, omitting 1 sc at end of last repeat, join with a slip stitch to first sc.
Round 5 Ch 3 (counts as first dc), 2 dc in first 3-ch sp, [3 dc in next 3-ch sp] twice, *[5 dc, ch 2, 5 dc] in next 6-ch sp, [3 dc in next 3-ch sp] 3 times; rep from * twice more, [5 dc, ch 2, 5 dc] in next 6-ch sp, join with a slip stitch to top of 3-ch. Fasten off.

To make patchwork blanket
Make 15 square motifs in each the following 14 colorways, for a total of 210 motifs:
Motif 1 Work each of these motifs in a single color—2 in mauve (A), 3 in light brown (B), 3 in gray (C), 2 in pale putty (D), 3 in turquoise (E), and 2 in dark brown (F).
Motif 2 Work these motifs in three colors—round 1 in turquoise (E), rounds 2–4 in pale putty (D), round 5 in dark brown (F).
Motif 3 Work these motifs in two colors—rounds 1–3 in pale putty (D), rounds 4 and 5 in mauve (A).
Motif 4 Work these motifs in three colors—rounds 1 and 2 in black (G), rounds 3 and 4 in pale putty

(D), round 5 in turquoise (E).

Motif 5 Work these motifs in three colors—round 1 in pale putty (D), round 2 in black (G), rounds 3–5 in mauve (A).

Motif 6 Work these motifs in two colors—rounds 1–4 in dark brown (F), round 5 in light brown (B).

Motif 7 Work these motifs in three colors—rounds 1 and 2 in mauve (A), round 3 in light brown (B), rounds 4 and 5 in dark brown (F).

Motif 8 Work these motifs in three colors—round 1 in dark brown (F), rounds 2 and 3 in turquoise (E), rounds 4 and 5 in pale putty (D).

Motif 9 Work these motifs in two colors—rounds 1 and 2 in turquoise (E), rounds 3–5 in light brown (B).

Motif 10 Work these motifs in three colors—rounds 1 and 2 in pale putty (D), rounds 3 and 4 in mauve (A), round 5 in gray (C).

Motif 11 Work these motifs in three colors—rounds 1 and 2 in gray (C), rounds 3 and 4 in black (G), round 5 in turquoise (E).

Motif 12 Work these motifs in four colors—round 1 in black (G), round 2 in gray (C), rounds 3 and 4 in turquoise (E), round 5 in light brown (B).

Motif 13 Work these motifs in three colors—round 1 in turquoise (E), rounds 2–4 in gray (C), round 5 in pale putty (D).

Motif 14 Work these motifs in two colors—rounds 1–4 in turquoise (E), round 5 in gray (C).

Masterclass

Arranging colored motifs for a patchwork effect

To create a patchwork-effect blanket, take your time when arranging the finished motifs. Lay them out on a flat surface in 15 rows of 14 motifs each. You will find that there are many pleasing arrangements possible; for example, you can arrange all the same motif colorways together to create blocks of color. In my arrangement, however, I was aiming for a soft, random effect. I used one square of each of the 14 colorways in each of the 15 rows of squares, making sure that the same colorways never touched.

To finish

Weave in any loose ends.
Lay motifs out flat and gently steam on wrong side.
Arrange the motifs into 15 rows of 14 squares (see masterclass).
Sew together the 14 squares in each of the 15 rows to form 15 strips, using small, neat overcast stitches and different colored yarns.
Then join the 15 strips together in the same way.
Edging
Using a C-2 (2.5mm) hook, work edging as follows:
Round 1 (RS) Using light brown (B), join yarn with a slip stitch to any dc along outside edge of blanket, ch 1, 1 sc in same dc as slip stitch, then work 1 sc in each dc, 1 sc in each space either side of seams joining the motifs together, and [1 sc, ch 1, 1 sc] in each blanket corner to end, join with a slip stitch to top of first sc. Fasten off.
Round 2 Using turquoise (E), join yarn with a slip stitch to any sc of previous round, ch 1, 1 sc in same sc as slip stitch, then work 1 sc in each sc, and [1 sc, ch 1, 1 sc] in each blanket corner to end, join with a slip stitch to top of first sc. Fasten off.
Round 3 Using black (G), rep round 2. Fasten off.

Stitch diagram Square Motif

KEY

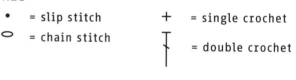

- = slip stitch   + = single crochet

○ = chain stitch   ⊤ = double crochet

Star tablecloth

This decorative centerpiece is made of repeated star motifs, multiplied to create a textile in which the negative spaces are as important as the positive shapes. The motifs are joined together as you work, leaving minimal finishing.

Skill level

EXPERIENCED

In this project you will learn
Joining shaped motifs as they are worked

Stitches used
Single crochet
Half double crochet
Double crochet

Size
Approximately 27$^{1}/_{2}$in/70cm in diameter

Materials
No. 10 linen crochet thread, such as Anchor Artiste Linen Crochet Thread No. 10 **2** FINE in one color:
   3 x 1$^{3}/_{4}$oz/50g balls (289yd/265m per ball)
   in natural
Size C-2 (2.5mm)crochet hook

Gauge
Each motif measures approximately 2$^{3}/_{4}$in/7cm in diameter using a C-2 (2.5mm) hook.

Abbreviation
See page 45.

To make tablecloth
The tablecloth is started at the center with a single star motif, then as the motifs are made they are joined onto the previous motifs. The diagrams show how the stars are added on—outward around the center in rounds.

Center star motif
Base ring Using a C-2 (2.5mm) hook, ch 9 and join with a slip stitch to first chain to form a ring.
Round 1 (RS) Ch 1, 18 sc in ring, join with a slip stitch to top of first sc.
Note: Do not turn at end of rounds but continue with RS of motif always facing.
Round 2 *Ch 9, 1 sc in 4th ch from hook, 1 hdc in each of next 2 ch, 1 dc in each of next 3 ch, skip next 2 sc on ring, 1 slip stitch in next sc; rep from * 5 times more, working last slip stitch in same sc as slip stitch on previous round.
Fasten off.

Stitch diagram Star
KEY

•	= slip stitch
○	= chain stitch
+	= single crochet
T	= half double crochet
𝒯	= double crochet

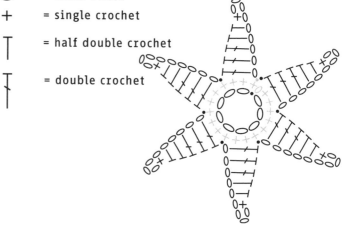

First round of motifs
Join the next six motifs to the center motif in a round around the center as shown in the diagrams as follows:
Work the first of these six motifs as for the center motif, but join the first two legs of this motif to the center motif as it is being worked. To do this, work the 9-ch of the first leg, carefully remove the hook from the loop and insert it through the 3-ch loop at the tip of one leg of the center motif, then pull the last loop of the 9-ch through the 3-ch loop and continue down the chain as instructed. Repeat this for the next leg, then finish the motif in the usual way.
Joining on motifs counterclockwise around the

center motif, work the second motif joining the first two legs to the center motif as before but also join the 3rd leg to the last leg worked on the first motif as shown on the diagram.

Repeat until you have attached six motifs all around the center motif, joining the last leg of the sixth motif to the third leg of the first motif in this round of motifs.

First motif of first round

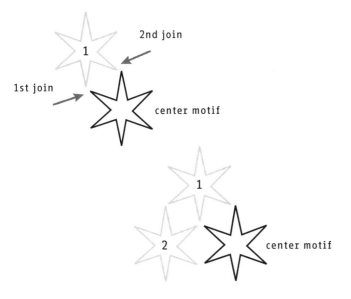

Star tablecloth Motif Placement

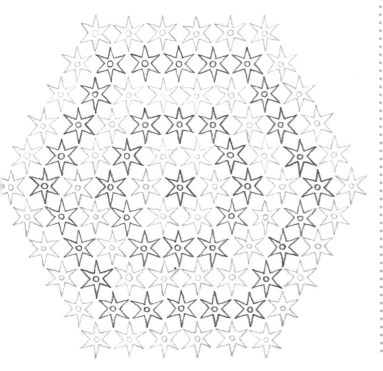

Remaining rounds of motifs

Continue making and joining on motifs in rounds around the center—join on 12 motifs in the second round, 18 in the third, 24 in the fourth, 30 in the fifth, and 36 in the sixth (the last round is not shown on the diagram below).

Note: Make sure you join the legs on the motifs to the legs of the adjacent motifs where they touch as shown in the diagram.

To finish

Weave in any loose ends.

Lay work out flat and gently steam on wrong side.

Masterclass

Crocheting motifs together

As well as avoiding having to sew countless motifs together, joining each motif at the connecting points means that you can build the overall shape of the textile as you work.

Make the center motif. Begin the first motif of the first round but join the first two legs to the center motif as it is being worked. To do this, work the 9 chain of the first leg, carefully remove the hook from the loop and insert it through the 3-chain loop at the tip of one leg of the center motif, then pull the last loop of the 9 chain through the 3-chain loop and continue down the chain as instructed. Repeat this for the next leg, then finish the motif in the usual way.

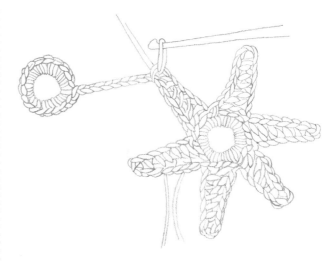

Asymmetrical cardigan

Nobody quite knows the origins of crochet but one of its earliest forms was as simulated lace, hence it was known as crochet lace or chain lace. For this throw-on cardigan, I have put a selection of crochet motifs under the microscope, enlarging them to create this overscaled lace design.

Skill level

⬤⬤⬤▬
EXPERIENCED

In this project you will learn
Joining random-shaped motifs
Working with super-bulky wool yarn

Stitches used
Single crochet; Half double crochet;
Double crochet; Double crochet bobbles;
Double crochet clusters

Size
One size
Finished measurements
Around bust 48in/122cm
Around sleeve 19in/48cm
Length from shoulder 23³/₄in/60cm
From sleeve edge to sleeve edge 44in/112cm

Materials
Super-bulky-weight wool yarn, such as erika knight Maxi Wool (**6**) SUPER BULKY in one color:
   9 x 3¹/₂oz/100g hanks (87yd/80m per hank) in ecru
Size N/P-15 (10mm) crochet hook
Large sheet of dressmaker's pattern paper

Gauges
Daisy bloom motif 7¹/₄in/18.5cm in diameter using an N/P-15 (10mm) hook.
Canterbury bell motif 4³/₄in/12cm in diameter using an N/P-15 (10mm) hook.
Wheel motif 5³/₄in/14.5cm in diameter using an N/P-15 (10mm) hook.
Small flower motif 4¹/₂in/11cm in diameter using an N/P-15 (10mm) hook.

Abbreviations
1 bobble = [yo and insert hook in sc, yo and draw a loop through, yo and draw through first 2 loops on hook] 5 times all in same sc, yo and draw a loop through all 6 loops on hook.
dc2tog = [yo and insert hook in next dc, yo and draw a loop through, yo and draw through first 2 loops on hook] twice, yo and draw a loop through all 3 loops on hook.
1 cluster = [yo and insert hook in 1-ch sp, yo and draw a loop through, yo and draw through first 2 loops on hook] 3 times all in same 1-ch sp, yo and draw a loop through all 4 loops on hook.
See also page 45.

Special note
The cardigan is made up of 59 motifs. The motifs are worked individually and then sewn together into the cardigan shape.

To make daisy bloom motif (make 16)

Base ring Using a N/P-15 (10mm) hook, ch 8 and join with a slip stitch to first chain to form a ring.

Round 1 (RS) Ch 3 (counts as first dc), 1 dc in ring, [ch 6, 3 dc in ring] 4 times, ch 6, 1 dc in ring, join with a slip stitch to top of 3-ch at beginning of round.

Note: Do not turn at end of rounds but continue with RS of motif always facing.

Round 2 *Ch 1, work [1 sc, 1 hdc, 7 dc, 1 hdc, 1 sc] all in next 6-ch sp, ch 1, skip 1 dc, 1 slip stitch in next dc (center dc of 3-dc group); rep from * 4 times more, working last slip stitch in top of 3-ch at beginning of previous round.
Fasten off.

Stitch diagram Daisy Bloom Motif

KEY

- • = slip stitch
- ○ = chain stitch
- + = double crochet
- ⊤ = half treble
- ╪ = treble crochet

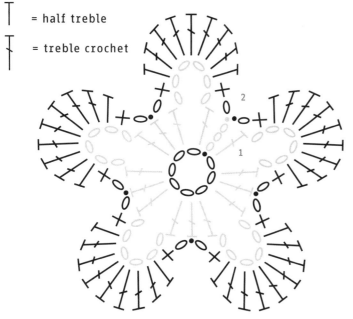

To make Canterbury bell motif (make 12)

Base ring Using an N/P-15 (10mm) hook, ch 6 and join with a slip stitch to first chain to form a ring.

Round 1 (RS) Ch 1, 12 sc in ring, join with a slip stitch to first sc.

Note: Do not turn at end of rounds but continue with RS of motif always facing.

Round 2 Ch 3, [yo and insert hook in same sc as last slip stitch, yo and draw a loop through, yo and draw through first 2 loops on hook] 4 times all in same place, yo and draw a loop through all 5 loops on hook (counts as first bobble), *ch 5, slip 1 sc, 1 bobble (see Abbreviations) in next sc; rep from * 4 times more, ch 5, join with a slip stitch to top of first bobble. Fasten off.

Stitch diagram Cantebury Bell Motif

KEY

- • = slip stitch
- ○ = chain stitch
- + = double crochet
- ⧫ = bobble

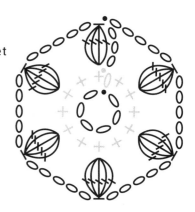

To make small flower motif (make 18)

Base ring Using an N/P-15 (10mm) hook, ch 6 and join with a slip stitch to first chain to form a ring.

Round 1 (RS) Ch 1, 15 sc in ring, join with a slip stitch to first sc.

Note: Do not turn at end of rounds but continue with RS of motif always facing.

Round 2 [ch 3, dc2tog over next 2 sc, ch 3, 1 slip stitch in next sc] 5 times, working last slip stitch in first sc of previous round.
Fasten off.

Stitch diagram Small Flower Motif

KEY

- • = slip stitch
- ○ = chain stitch
- + = double crochet
- ⋀ = tr2tog

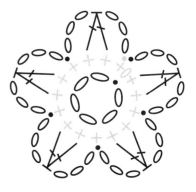

To make wheel motif (make 13)

Base ring Using a N/P-15 (10mm) hook, ch 4 and join with a slip stitch to first chain to form a ring.

Round 1 (RS) Ch 4 (counts as first dc and a 1-ch sp), [1 dc, ch 1] 11 times in ring, 1 slip stitch in 3rd of 4-ch at beginning of round.

Note: Do not turn at end of rounds but continue with RS of motif always facing.

Round 2 1 slip stitch under next ch (the first 1-ch sp), ch 3, [yo and insert hook in 1-ch sp, yo and draw a loop through, yo and draw through first 2 loops on hook] twice all in same 1-ch sp as last slip st, yo and draw a loop through all 3 loops on hook (counts as first cluster), [ch 3, 1 cluster (see page 133) in next 1-ch sp] 11 times, ch 3, join with a slip stitch to top of first cluster.

Fasten off.

Stitch diagram Wheel Motif

KEY

- • = slip stitch
- ○ = chain stitch
- ⟙ = treble crochet
- ⬨ = cluster

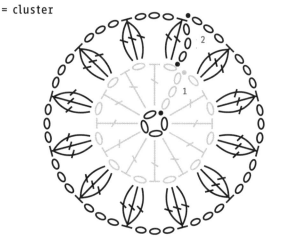

To finish cardigan

Weave in any loose ends.

Lay motifs out flat and gently steam motifs on wrong side.

Following the dimensions on the diagram, draw the cardigan shape on a sheet of dressmaker's pattern paper. Position the motifs right side up on top of the paper pattern shape as indicated on the diagram and as close together as possible—nudge the motifs into shapes that allow them to fit together tightly and touch their neighbors. Pin the motifs in position on the paper.

Sew the motifs together with overcast stitches, leaving all the motifs pinned to the paper until you have finished sewing them together. Remember to leave a opening about 10″ long at the center for the neck opening and from the neck to the bottom edge on the front for the cardigan opening.

Remove the pins and sew the side and sleeve seams with right sides together.

Masterclass

Meshing motifs together

Motifs are deceptively pliable when it comes to meshing them together to make a larger piece, such as this cruciform shape that makes up the cardigan. Always work on a flat, clean surface such as a table. I don't recommend using the floor as carpets and other floor coverings can create an uneven surface. Before sewing them together, lightly steam each motif to enhance the yarn and highlight the individual shapes. Once all the motifs are laid out, squish them together to achieve the required overall shape. At each connecting point, oversew the motifs together. There will undoubtedly be a few adjustments necessary.

Asymmetrical cardigan
Motif Placement

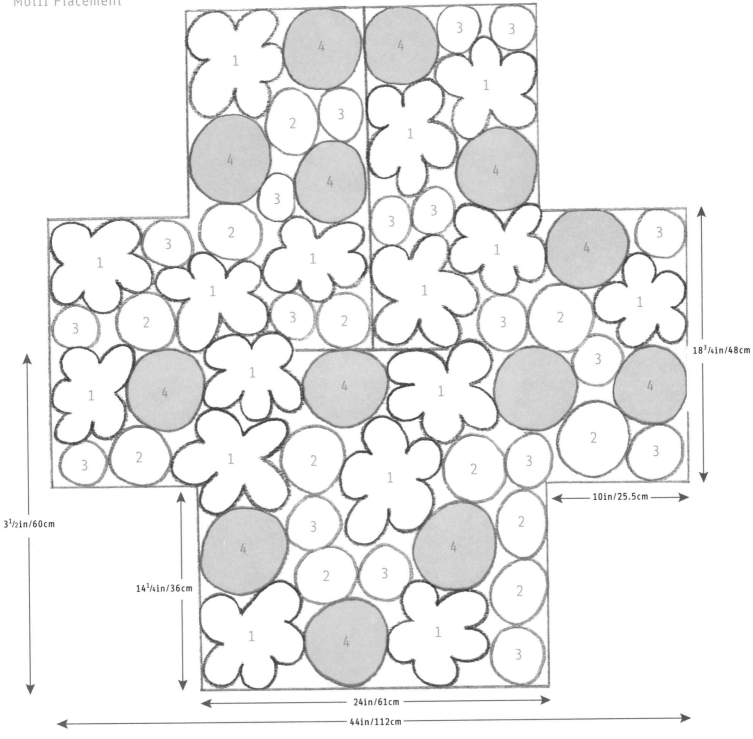

18³/₄in/48cm

10in/25.5cm

23¹/₂in/60cm

14¹/₄in/36cm

24in/61cm

44in/112cm

KEY

1 = daisy bloom motif
2 = canterbury bell motif
3 = small flower motif
4 = wheel motif

Edging stitch scarf

Many crochet stitches are used to add decorative edges to textiles. I have taken a fresh look at edgings, working one of my favorite "popcorn" stitches in a chunky yarn to create a long pretty scarf to wear wrapped around the neck.

Skill level

EXPERIENCED

In this project you will learn
Working popcorns, see masterclass on page 141
Working a heading along an edging

Stitches used
Single crochet; Double crochet;
Double crochet popcorns

Size
Approximately 4¼in/10.5cm wide x 75in/190cm long

Materials
Bulky-weight wool yarn, such as erika knight Vintage Wool ⑤ BULKY in one color:
  4 x 1¾oz/50g hanks (95yd/87m per hank) in ecru
Sizes H-8 (5mm) and I-9 (5.5mm) crochet hooks

Gauge
Working to an exact gauge is not essential for this project.

Abbreviations
1 popcorn at beginning of row = ch 3, work 6 dc in first sp, remove loop from hook and insert hook from front through top of 3-ch, pick up dropped loop and draw it through, ch 1 to secure popcorn.
1 popcorn = work 7 dc in next sp, remove loop from hook and insert hook from front through top of first of these 7-dc, pick up dropped loop and draw it through, ch 1 to secure popcorn.
See also page 45.

To make scarf
The edging is worked in a strip of half-circle motifs, then the heading is added along one edge.
Edging
Base ring Using an I-9 (5.5mm) hook, ch 10 and join with a slip stitch to first chain to form a ring.
Row 1 (RS) Ch 3 (counts as first dc), 14 dc in ring, turn.
Row 2 Ch 5 (counts as 1 dc and ch 2), skip first 2 dc, 1 dc in next dc, [ch 2, skip 1 dc, 1 dc in next dc] 6 times, working last dc of last repeat in 3rd of 3-ch at end of row, turn.
Work popcorns across next row, making the first popcorn as explained in Abbreviations and the remaining 6 popcorns with 7-dc in normal way, as follows:
Row 3 (popcorn row) Work 1 popcorn at beginning of row, [ch 3, 1 popcorn in next 2-ch sp] 6 times, working last popcorn of last repeat in 5-ch sp, turn.
Row 4 Ch 10, skip first 2 sps, work [1 sc, ch 5, 1 sc] all in next 3-ch sp, turn.
Row 5 Ch 3 (counts as first dc), 14 dc in 5-ch sp, turn.
Repeat rows 2–5 until work measures 75in/190cm from beginning, ending with a row 3 (a popcorn row)—but do not fasten off and do not turn at end of last row.
Heading
Continue along side edge with RS facing and work heading as follows:
Heading row 1 Ch 3, 1 sc in 5-ch sp formed at beg of row 2 of pattern, *ch 5, 1 sc in 10-ch sp formed at beg of row 4 of pattern, ch 5, 1 sc in 5-ch sp formed at beg of row 2 of pattern; rep from * to end, turn.
Heading row 2 Ch 1, 1 sc in first sc, *5 sc in next 5-ch sp, 1 sc in next sc; rep from * to end, turn. Change to an H-8 hook.
Heading row 3 Ch 1, 1 sc in first st, *ch 3, skip 1 st, 1 sc in next st; rep from * to end.
Fasten off.

To finish
Weave in any loose ends.
Lay scarf out flat and steam very gently on wrong side.

Masterclass

The stitch pattern used for this scarf includes popcorn stitches.

Working popcorn stitch
Popcorn stitches add raised texture to otherwise flat surfaces.

1 When you come to the first popcorn row on the scarf (row 3), begin by working 3 chain.

2 Work 6 doubles into the first 2-chain space of the previous row.

3 Carefully drop the loop from the hook and insert the hook from the front to the back through the top of the 3-chain at the beginning of the row.

4 Then pick up the dropped loop.

5 Draw the loop through the chain.

6 Work 1 chain to secure the "popcorn."

7 Work 3 chain, then work 7 doubles into the next space. Drop the loop from the hook.

8 Insert the hook from the front through the top of the first of these 7 doubles, pick up the dropped loop then complete and secure the "popcorn" as before. Work the following 7-dc popcorns of the row in the same way.

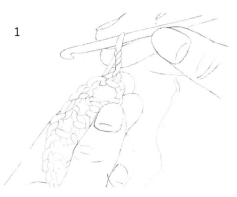

1

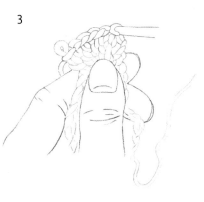

3

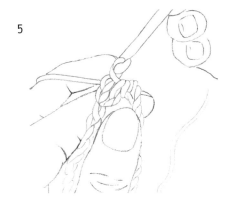

5

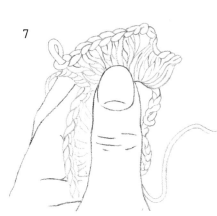

7

2

4

6

8

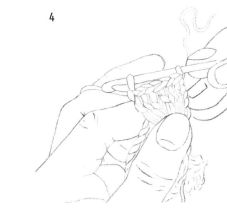

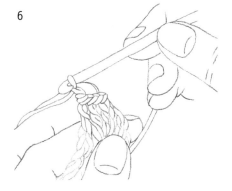

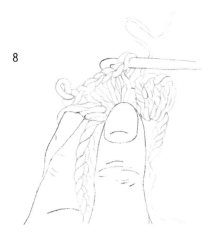

Recommended yarns

There is a yarn specified for each of the designs in the Project Workshops section of this book. If you are sticking to the recommended yarn, just pick your preferred shade. However, if you are using a different yarn to that specified you must compare the gauges given to ensure the finished result will not wildly differ.

There are standard weights—or thicknesses—of yarns, recognized throughout the industry. Hand-knit yarns commonly range from 4-ply or fingering through double knitting or sport weight to super bulky at the opposite end of the scale. Within each of these categories there is a degree of tolerance, so it is important to check the gauge of each yarn against that given in a pattern (see Checking Your Gauge, page 41).

Each yarn will have slightly varying physical properties from the next and will perform differently. Some yarns may be colorfast and easycare whilst others may only be suitable for drycleaning or could possibly felt if not treated correctly. The care information for a yarn will be given on the yarn wrapped that comes wrapped around a ball, hank, or skein. I always keep a yarn wrapper for each project that I make—and if I give a hand knit as a gift, I include the yarn wrapper so the recipient knows how to care for the item. When you invest so much of your time and energy into creating a hand-made item, great care should be taken in the laundering.

Alongside the manufacturer's brand and the name given to the specific yarn, a yarn wrapper will typically carry the following information:

Recommended gauge and hook/needle sizes
This is the recommended gauge and hook or needle size, however a designer may vary from this recommendation within a pattern. If so, always go with the designer's recommendation.

Weight of yarn
Given in ounces in the US and grams in the UK, most yarns come in either $1^3/_4$oz/50g or $3^1/_2$oz/100g balls.

Yardage
This is the approximate length of yarn in the ball and is just as important to consider as gauge when considering a substitute yarn.

Fiber composition
A yarn wrapper will list the materials that the yarn is made from, whether that is 100% pure wool or a blend of fibers such as cotton and silk. This affects not just the method of care for the finished item, but also the suitability of a yarn for a certain project.

Shade and dye-lot numbers
Each shade of yarn is given an identifying name and/or number by the manufacturer. When purchasing yarn the dye-lot number is equally, if not more important, as this number needs to be the same on every ball. As yarn is dyed in batches, buying yarn with the same dye-lot numbers ensures there will be no color variations between balls.

Care instructions
A yarn wrapper will indicate whether the yarn is suitable for machine washing or is dry clean only, and whether or not it can be ironed and, if so, at what temperature. This information is usually given in the form of standard care symbols.

Anchor Artiste Linen Crochet Thread No.10
A fine-weight linen yarn; 100% pure linen; 289yd/265m per $1^3/_4$oz/50g; recommended crochet hook size—6 steel to B-1.

Erika Knight Maxi Wool
A super-bulky-weight wool yarn; 100% pure wool; 87yd/80m per $3^1/_2$oz/100g; recommended crochet hook size—N/P-15 (10mm).

Erika Knight Vintage Wool
A bulky-weight wool yarn; 100% pure wool; 95yd/87m per $1^3/_4$oz/50g; recommended crochet hook size—H-8 (5mm) to I-9 (5.5mm).

Ingrid Wagner Big Knit Yarn
A thrum yarn consisting of a continuous 1in-/2.5cm-wide strip of patterned woven wool fabric—an industrial selvage edge; 100% pure wool; 23yd/21m per $17^1/_2$oz/500g; recommended crochet hook size—U (25mm).

Rowan Baby Alpaca DK
A light double-knitting-weight alpaca yarn; 100% baby alpaca; 109yd/100m per $1^3/_4$oz/50g; recommended crochet hook size—G-6 (4mm).

Rowan Cashsoft 4-Ply
A super-fine-weight cashmere-merino blend yarn; 10% cashmere, 57% extra-fine merino wool, 33% acrylic microfiber; 175yd/160m per $1^3/_4$oz/50g; recommended crochet hook size—C-2 to D-3 (3mm).

Rowan Cotton Glacé
A fine-weight cotton yarn; 100% cotton; 126yd/115m per $1^3/_4$oz/50g; recommended crochet hook size—D-3 to F-5 (3.25mm to 3.75mm).

Rowan Fine Lace
A lace-weight alpaca-merino blend yarn; 80% baby suri alpaca, 20% fine merino wool; 437yd/400m per $1^3/_4$oz/50g; recommended crochet hook size—B-1 to G-6 (2mm to 4mm).

Rowan Handknit Cotton
A double-knitting-weight cotton yarn; 100% cotton; 93yd/85m per $1^3/_4$oz/50g; recommended crochet hook size—G-6 to H-8 (4mm to 4.5mm).

Rowan Lenpur Linen
A double-knitting-weight linen blend yarn; 75% viscose, 25% linen; 126yd/115m per $1^3/_4$oz/50g; recommended crochet hook size—G-6 (4mm).

Rowan Lima
An aran-weight alpaca-merino blend yarn; 84% alpaca, 8% merino, 8% nylon; 109yd/100m per $1^3/_4$oz/50g; recommended crochet hook size—I-9 (5.5mm).

Rowan Purelife British Sheep Breeds Chunky Undyed
A bulky-weight wool yarn; 100% pure wool; 120yd/110m per $3^1/_2$oz/100g; recommended crochet hook size—K10$^1/_2$ to L-11 (7mm).

Rowan Savannah
An aran-weight cotton-silk blend yarn; 94% cotton, 6% silk; 87yd/80m per $1^3/_4$oz/50g; recommended crochet hook size—H-8 (5mm).

Yeoman's Cotton Cannele 4-Ply
A super-fine-weight cotton yarn; 100% mercerized cotton; 957yd/875m per $8^3/_4$oz/245g; recommended crochet hook size—C-2 (2.75mm).

Templates for slipper boots
(see pages 92–95)

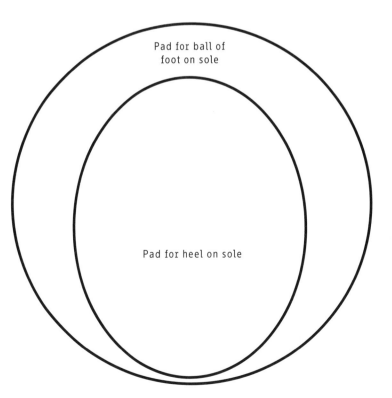

Pad for ball of foot on sole

Pad for heel on sole

Acknowledgments

Once again the simple ethos of the projects in this book belies the complex nature of putting a title like this together. I have been privileged to work with some of the publishing and craft world's best professionals, experts of the highest calibre with the most discerning eyes, meticulous attention to detail, and above all unbelievable patience, for which I am forever grateful. I would like to extend my enormous appreciation for their contributions. This book would certainly not have happened without them.

The truly fabulous team at Quadrille Publishing. To my Publisher and Editorial Director, Alison Cathie and Jane O'Shea. To my project editor Lisa Pendreigh — my sincerest thanks for her professionalism, exceptional patience and personal support—as well as designers Claire Peters and Nicola Davidson for their creative and yet exacting design. And to Aysun Hughes for doing such a fabulous job in the production of the book.

It has been a thrill to work again with photographer Yuki Sugiura; her natural sense of style is central to the sensibility of this book. And, of course, Kim for assisting. My thanks, too, to our stylist Charis for her diligence in the detail. And not forgetting the adorable Panda for so beautifully modelling the pet bed.

To my brilliant project maker, problem solver, and personal friend Sally Lee; I am enormously grateful for her misspent—or rather well-spent—youth crafting, knitting, sewing, and making stuff. And, of course, to Sally Harding, for her meticulous work in pattern checking.

As people who know me will testify, I pour over each and every detail endlessly. The choice of yarn is always paramount to me, but most especially when designing and offering projects of simple design. Hence my sincerest thanks and appreciation to the following creators of exceptional yarns of rare distinction for their generosity and enthusiastic support: Rowan, the iconic yarn brand, Anchor, Ingrid Wagner, and Yeoman's Yarns for constantly producing desirable fibers and yarns of excellent quality which entice and excite the creative soul. Long may you continue to do so.

Finally I dedicate this book to creatives and crafters everywhere, especially to the new breed of artisan entrepreneurs who are emerging and growing in number and confidence: who continually excite with their passion for the handmade, who constantly push the boundaries of craft with their enthusiasm, innovation, and origination.

Publisher's Acknowledgments

The publisher would like to thank the following for loaning accessories and other items:

LAUREN DENNEY
www.laurendenney.com

ERCOL
www.ercol.com